D1404667

SPACES FOR LIVING

SPACES FOR LIVING

How to create multifunctional rooms for today's homes

LIZ BAUWENS AND ALEXANDRA CAMPBELL

Photography by Simon Brown

CLARKSON POTTER/PUBLISHERS

NEW YORK

To Frederick, Rosalind, Lois, Milo and Finn

Copyright © 1999 by Collins & Brown Limited
Text copyright © 1999 by Liz Bauwens and Alexandra Campbell
Photographs copyright © 1999 by Collins & Brown Limited

All rights reserved. No part of this publication may be reproduced or transmitted
in any form or by any means, electronic or mechanical, including photocopying,
recording, or by any information storage and retrieval system, without permission
in writing from the publisher.

Published by Clarkson N. Potter/Publishers, 201 East 50th Street, New York,
New York 10022.
Member of the Crown Publishing Group

Random House, Inc. New York, Toronto, London, Sydney, Auckland
www.randomhouse.com

CLARKSON N. POTTER, POTTER, and colophon are trademarks of
Clarkson N. Potter, Inc.

Originally published in Great Britain by Collins & Brown Limited in 1999.

Reproduced by Grafiscan, Verona Italy
Printed and bound in Hong Kong by Dai Nippon Printing Co.

Editor: Mary Lambert
Designer: Christine Wood
Illustrator: Kate Simunek

Library of Congress Cataloging-in-Publication Data

Bauwens, Liz
Spaces for living: how to create multifunctional rooms for today's home/
Liz Bauwens and Alexandra Campbell—1st American ed.
Includes index
1. Room layout (Dwellings) 2. Interior decoration. I. Campbell, Alexandra
II. Title.
NL2113.B38 1999
747.7—dc21   98-26900

ISBN: 0-609-89899-X (hard cover)
ISBN: 0-609-80355-7 (paperback)

10 9 8 7 6 5 4 3 2 1

First American Edition

contents

introduction

Spaces for Living is about the way we live now. Dual-purpose rooms and open-plan layouts mean that the walls have come down between formal and informal parts of the house, between friends and family, and, as increasing numbers of people work from home for at least part of the time, between our social and professional lives. It's a more relaxed way of living but often a more pressured life – with space and time at a premium, houses must not only look good, but make optimum use of the available space and be easy to live in. We are both working mothers with busy lives, we have offices at home, enjoy entertaining and family life, and have ever-growing demands for good storage solutions. Yet we also want to live in houses that reflect our personalities.

The houses and apartments featured on the following pages are all real homes, and every photograph reflects a real answer to the dilemmas presented when decorating today. Some of the

homes have been designed by professionals, others by those who live in

them, many by a combination of the two. Some are large houses, while

others are exceptionally small.

Interiors today rival fashion as showcases for personal style, so these are

design-led solutions to the common problems of creating a home that feels

as good as it looks, yet they are equally appropriate to those on a tight

budget or to more lavish projects. Tastes range from those who collect

antiques to the more vibrantly modern, yet all reflect an individual attitude to style. Some are family homes, others are lived in by one or two people, but they are all twenty-four hour living spaces, where people live, work, sleep, and play, rather

than places which are merely dormitories at the end of the day. They are interiors that make it easy to talk — in this high-pressure, fast-lane world, there's often all too little time

to communicate. Yet privacy is also an issue in an over-crowded world, so space is also carved out for peace and relaxation.

Spaces for Living offers many answers to these contradictory, contemporary questions, and whether you are buying just one item to update a room, or renovating a whole house, here are ideas and solutions that will make it work. Between us we have over thirty years' experience in interiors and design on magazines, and we learned a great deal while researching and writing this book. We hope you will too.

Liz Bauwens

Alexandra Campbell

KITCHEN

PLUS

The kitchen as the "heart of the home" has become a cliché – but only because it is so true. People are prepared to spend significant sums to ensure that it is comfortable, practical and reflects their lifestyle. Today most kitchens do have some sort of dual-purpose function, frequently doubling up as dining rooms, play areas, or living zones.

Today's kitchen requires new thinking: does it belong in a bigger or better room in the house? Is it really practical to have the units round the sides and the table in the middle? Think in terms of "work zones": the wet zone (sink and dishwasher), the cooking area (cooktop, oven, food chopping area) and even a refreshment zone (coffee, kettle, cups). Store everything according to zone, and make sure all have easy access to water. You should also be able to move around the room easily, and everyday items should be more accessible than special-occasion silverware, china and glassware.

the city kitchen/ dining room

This spacious, light room was originally the formal living room of a family home, while the kitchen was crammed into a small room at the back. By reassessing the way their home and lifestyle interact, this family transformed their living quarters with a large kitchen-dining room, making it into a busy family room as well as the focal point of the house. This then released other space for relaxation and living.

This kitchen-dining room is smart enough for formal entertaining, and the well-equipped kitchen has plenty of space for food preparation, cooking, and storage.

The central island makes it a sociable room, where the cook is part of the conversation whether he or she is preparing a family meal or a dinner party for friends.

a fresh look

The success of this room is due to the way the family re assessed their lifestyle after years of living in the house. It had originally been laid out according to the traditions of 100 years ago when it was built, so a twentieth-century lifestyle was trying to exist in a nineteenth-century building. The main issue was the kitchen, a small room off the living room. Because family and friends congregated in the kitchen, the large, beautiful living room was left unoccupied. A separate dining room was also underused. After much thought, plus a feng shui consultation from architect and feng shui practitioner Christian Kyriacou, they decided to use the biggest room for the kitchen-diner, turn the dining room into a smaller formal living room, and transform the kitchen into a television room cum den. Now the kitchen-dining room is the biggest and best-situated room – and, as in feng shui terms it falls into the "relationships" area of the house, it has become the perfect place for everyone to congregate. The whole building flows better, because instead of cramming 80 percent of family life into 25 percent of the floor space, daily activities can be spread out through virtually the whole ground floor.

the dining area

Here a Fifties' Wurlitzer jukebox adds a lively note and draws attention to the fun part of the room. There are just two or three substantial pieces of furniture: a dining table, glass-front cabinet, and fireplace. The cabinet is, in fact, a set of mahogany library shelves, and, because the wood was so good, the family debated on whether to paint it. It was resolved, and once painted white, everybody realized that it had been worth trusting their instincts.

The room was painted Standard White, a white that is slightly less crisp than Brilliant White. To add a little more definition, a very slightly darker shade was used for the woodwork of the units, the coves, and the baseboards. Such a shade variation is scarcely detectable to many, but it helps to give shape and some definition to a large expanse of one color.

1: Storing glasses behind the glass doors shows them off to advantage, and keeps the dresser looking calm and uncluttered.

2: A 1950s' jukebox provides a colourful focus in an otherwis monochrome scheme, and it plays great records too.

right: The dining end of the room.

the kitchen

This room has two big windows, large French doors onto th garden, a fireplace, and two internal doors, one leading to the de and the other to the main hallway. This means that ther is comparatively little wall space for full-length cabinets especially as a large fridge-freezer and a family-size range take u a substantial part of the main wall. The solution, designed b architect Christopher Spink, was to have built-in kitchen cabinet at waist height extending out into the room as a breakfas

ar cum room divider, providing generous work surfaces and plenty of under-counter storage. This separates the dining and eating areas, with the fireplace, table, and glass-front cabinet in one half of the room, and all the kitchen equipment in the other. The arrangement fitted in well with the feng shui aspect of the brief too, as the owners were advised to make a very clear division between the two uses of the room.

A central island creates more storage space and work surfaces, housing the dishwasher, and providing a useful place to hang

radiators. One of its drawers contains pots and pans, conveniently close to the range, while the drawer mechanism means that pots are easy to locate without having to search around at the backs of cabinets. Central islands, one of the most popular introductions in kitchens over the past decade, work particularly well in big rooms such as this, because they offer the cook the chance to face into the room while he or she is working, to take part in any conversation that is going on, or to keep an eye on young children. In a big room they also cut down on time spent walking

■ A breakfast bar is good as a room divider, creating extra work surfaces and storage. It also keeps children and pets away from the cooking area. However, it reduces flexibility because it is built-in so you can't clear the room for special occasions.

■ A central island is sociable, offering an extra work surface within easy reach of stove, sink, and cupboards, and extra space beneath for storage. However, it takes up far more space than most people realize, and can be an obstacle in small spaces.

■ Most kitchens need some built-in elements to maximize the space, but don't just accept a standard layout. Think through the preparation of a typical family meal, special-occasion cooking, and even a snack or cup of coffee. Work out where you'll keep everything and whether things are in easy reach.

■ Deep drawers often work better than cabinets because you can pull them out and get at everything easily, rather than rooting around at the back to find pots or pans.

from one side to the other, and mean that you can cook with everything in easy reach. However, in smaller kitchens, they can be something of an obstacle.

The fridge-freezer was encased in a larger frame, with storage space above, while open corner shelves provide more storage areas. To avoid a closed-off feeling, the cabinets stop short of the ceiling, something that works very successfully in a room with high ceilings, and impressive pediments were added on top to create a sense of proportion. The placing of the sink works well in functional terms, but its position was also dictated by feng shui – the sink is by the window because windows and glass are both water elements and it is considered wise to keep the water function close by.

lighting

Lighting is very important in any dual-purpose room, and here the low-voltage spotlights set into the ceiling on two different circuits insure that the dining and kitchen areas can be lit separately. Natural daylight was an issue too – although there are French doors opening onto a terrace and large windows facing the garden, it's a north-facing room, so a skylight was added, and now sunlight floods into the room all year around. The white paint, plus the use of a relatively pale wood – maple – for the countertop, along with pale, natural wood floors, all also add to the impression of good natural light.

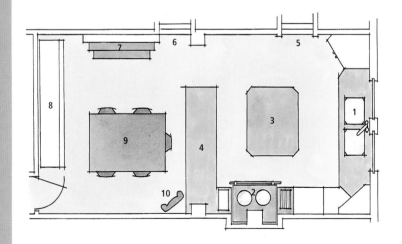

FLOORPLAN
(1) Sink facing window.
(2) Cooking range. (3) Central island, including radiators.
(4) Breakfast bar. (5) Doors to garden. (6) Door to TV room.
(7) Fireplace. (8) Mahogany glass-front cabinet painted white. (9) Dining table.
(10) Jukebox.

A black granite backsplash gives the range a sleek, sophisticated look. There is also a ceramic cooktop (1) next to it to provide additional cooking facilities or to use in the height of summer when the range (an Aga, which is permanently warm) is switched off. The central island (2) has drawers containing pots and pans facing the range, with a radiator hung on each side and a dishwasher enclosed on the fourth side. This big corner of the breakfast bar (3) is either used for eating, or as a decorative focal point with a big vase of flowers.

the kitchen/ playroom

This stylish L-shaped kitchen-playroom is also a dining room. Well designed storage means that everything can be hidden away after use, while flexible furniture offers a combination of options. Two tables on wheels can become either a dining table plus work surface or an extra-long table or they can be rolled aside. All equipment, such as the toaster and the blender, is hidden behind cabinet doors which can be opened for use when in place.

These custom-built cabinets are the key to the success of this adaptable room. At the playroom end they conceal toys, books, china, and the TV.

The two matching ones situated on either side of the cooking range contain food, utensils, and electrical equipment for use in the kitchen.

The working zone

This kitchen is sleek and stylish, but still a warm, friendly family room. In many ways, it is the ultimate contemporary example of a room that doesn't feel like a kitchen. It is a design that aims to conceal, and it is the antithesis of the traditional family kitchen with its hanging pots, hutch with plates on display, and kettle permanently on the boil. The owner was determined that everything could be put away, so the kitchen was built to conceal the clutter of food preparation. When all the cabinet doors are closed, only the big range gives clues as to the room's real function. Above all, the owner wanted to be able to put everything out of sight quickly and easily, so that the family never had to look at toasters, kettles, or food processors while they relaxed or played at the other end of the room. Crucial to this was the knowledge that taking things out of cabinets, plugging them in, and then putting them away again was likely to prove too much with a busy life and small children around.

Each cabinet, therefore, is virtually a mini kitchen area of its own, with special sections to house electrical equipment, where each piece can be left permanently plugged in. A pull-out shelf directly underneath extends outward when the cabinet door is opened, offering a work surface for bowls, pots, or pans. Once

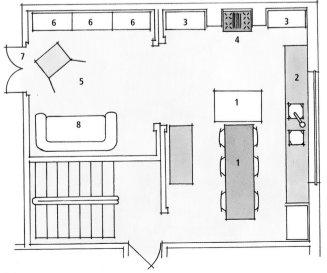

FLOORPLAN
(1) Tables on wheels that can be placed at right angles or in one line. (2) Run of kitchen cabinets with sink. (3) Cabinets housing food and plugged-in electrical equipment, including pull-out work surfaces.
(4) Range. (5) Play area.
(6) Coordinating cabinets housing toys, books, TV, VCR and music system. (7) Doors to garden. (8) Sofa.

above: The cabinets open up to reveal equipment such as a plugged-in food processor, ice-cream maker, and toaster, each with its own pull-out work surface.

above: There are no obvious kitchen cabinets above the height of the work surface. The white and steel decorative theme is easy to live with and is visually consistent; the refrigerator handles are echoed on the cabinets (1). The steel-edged range (2) is modern, but adds a welcoming feel to the room. Stainless steel sinks (3) give stylish practicality for food preparation and washing dishes.

the toast is buttered or the soup blended, it takes only seconds to take away the plate or pot, slide the work surface back into the cabinet and close the door. Very little space is wasted, because the shelves above have been carefully measured to make the most of every available space, and items can be kept close to the place where they will be used: teas, coffees, and sugars near the kettle, jams close to the toaster, and spices near the food processor.

This policy reduces the need for a run of standard kitchen cabinets. It really is not possible to hide the sink and drainer, so a short run of cabinets incorporating these and housing the dishwasher, plus some extra storage, has been placed just in front of the window. Even that has been visually minimized as much as

THE KITCHEN/ PLAYROOM CHECKLIST

■ Decide what the cabinets will hold before building them. Simply installing as many standard cabinets as possible will not necessarily be the best option. Children can tidy up from an early age if it is clear where things go.

■ Build in flexibility, especially in shelving. Boxes of bulky toddler toys will be replaced by games, model-making kits, books, and videos in only a few years.

■ Children need space to play, so keep any furniture to a minimum.

■ Conceal all wires and keep electrical equipment out of reach of toddlers. Having equipment hidden away, as in this kitchen-playroom, is safe as well as stylish. Lighting is built-in, with low-voltage halogen spots on a dimmer switch, so there are no table lamps to be pulled over. Make sure that children are not able to pull pans off the stove.

■ Use easy-to-clean, hard-wearing materials, such as wipe-clean flooring and washable paintwork or upholstery slipcovers.

left: The two tables on wheels at right angles to each other, make a breakfast table and a work surface, but they can easily be swung around to make one extra-long table.

1: The chairs were chosen to fi into the contemporary feel of the scheme.

possible, with a single sleek faucet housed discreetly over a white sink and drainer.

The two other "kitcheny" items, are, of course, the refrigerator and the cooking range, and these too have been incorporated subtly into the visual scheme. By using a discreet steel theme (steel edging or steel panels for the cabinets), the stainless steel family fridge and the steel-edged range blend in without looking aggressively industrial or too conspicuous.

Apart from these cabinets, the major items of furniture in this room are two tables on wheels. Both are exactly the same height and width, although they are different lengths. They are usually put at right angles to each other, with one providing a convenient work surface in front of the range, and the other acting as a family kitchen table. However, occasionally there is a big dinner

2 and 3: The cabinets open to reveal adjustable shelves for toys, kept at a height that means even toddlers can learn about tidying up. In future years these could hold books, games, videos, or other toys. They also cleverly conceal the TV, VCR, and a music system.

right: With just one sofa along one wall there is plenty of play space to set up train sets and dollhouses. The cream linen draperies have been "toddler-proofed" with a very broad band of darker linen at the base, so that sticky fingers can draw the drapes without leaving obvious marks.

for family Sunday lunch, and the two tables are swung around to run together down the entire length of the kitchen and playroom area. This means that as many as 16 friends and family members can be entertained together in convivial circumstances.

the playing zone

The play area part of the L shape has direct access onto the garden through French doors, which can be opened in the summer so that children can easily run in and out of the garden under the eye of an adult.

This section of the room is not very wide, and it has been deliberately kept as clear of furniture as possible in order to provide the maximum amount of space for the children to play with different toys, paint, set up a railway track, or push around

a toddle truck. A sofa placed against one wall provides a comfortable seating area for some story-reading or for watching children's television.

Once again, the cabinets are the key to keeping the room calm and well organized, even when there are small children constantly moving around. First they tie in visually with the kitchen cabinetry, signaling a change of priorities by reversing the steel and white theme with steel panels instead of edging. The lower cupboards contain toys that the children can easily reach themselves, while precious china and glass is kept at the higher levels out of the reach of tiny hands. The television is also concealed in the cabinets, on a swing arm so that it pulls in and out smoothly. When not in use it is easily hidden from children and also from any visitors.

the country kitchen/ dining room

This kitchen-dining room is a newly built extension to a 200-year-old cottage, and is the cottage's biggest and busiest room. The owners were meticulous about keeping the cottage's atmosphere in the new part, using old bricks in its construction and paying attention to details such as windows and doors, but they also wanted to live a contemporary twentieth-century family life in it. The brief was to make it stylish, yet in tune with a period building.

There is a casual, contemporary feel to this country kitchen because the style and color of each run of fitted cabinets is different. They are all simple, but with discreet touches such as the doors with carved hearts and initials. The color is echoed in the bright, mixed china in the dining area (inset).

The brief

Although this kitchen is in a new addition, the owners wanted it to be in tune with a period building and a country lifestyle, while being stylish, comfortable, and contemporary. The first thing to consider was that, because the owners wanted one spacious room to open up the whole house, the room would be larger than any of the cottage's original rooms. The dimensions were restricted by what local ordinances would allow in an old cottage of that size – often, local ordinances or restrictive covenants will only allow additions up to a certain size. The owners decided that all the extra space would be dedicated to the kitchen-dining room.

Second, they resolved the issue of how to combine historical detail and twentieth-century life with a few clever concealing tricks. Full-length doors open out onto the garden in the summer, but instead of making these glass French doors, the decision was taken to make them stable doors with solid wooden halves below the glass. This maintains the size of the new windows so that they are in keeping with the period ones in the rest of the house, while opening the room up to the garden on sunny days.

FLOORPLAN
(1) Range. (2) Built-in shelves and cabinets. (3) Armoire for refrigerator and food. (4) Blue cabinets with chest of drawers between. (5) Run of cabinets by sink. (6) Hutch. (7) Work table. (8) Dining table. (9) Doors leading to garden.

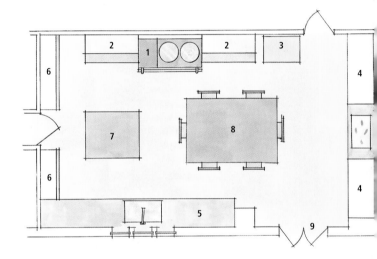

ll the new windows and latches were handmade to mirror those f the cottage. When the newness has worn off, it will not be ossible to tell which doors and windows were made in the ventieth century and which in the eighteenth.

isguising equipment

ishwasher, microwave and blender are all hidden away in abinets, but are easily accessible. A combination of built-in and reestanding furniture was chosen – the built-in because, with so ttle space elsewhere, it was essential to store everything in one om, and the freestanding to give it a more relaxed country feel. he cabinets are painted in a rainbow of different colors, yet held gether by a disciplined design eye, to insure that the room looks olorful, rather than over-matched.

The range strikes a homey note, surrounded by all the pots, ans, and drawers that are needed for cooking. The pans hang om a rail beside this stove, which means that they are within rm's reach – a great bonus for a busy mother. There is an unusual ombination of drawers, cabinets, and shelves, with drawers on level with the range, and mainly shelves above. This gives he whole combination the feel of a traditional Welsh dresser,

1: Drawers are divided into compartments for easy access.

2: Different-size shelving makes the best use of the available space.

3: The stove backsplash is painted with hard-wearing acrylic paint, rather than being decorated with the usual tiles.

4: All cooking utensils are housed near the range.

5: The bold pink window shade adds some zest to the softer pastel colors in the kitchen.

6: Carved inset hearts and initials are a simple decorative element on some of the kitchen cabinets.

although the simplicity of the woodwork and knobs makes it a very contemporary solution. Surprisingly, there is no tiled backsplash to protect the paintwork around the range – just ordinary acrylic paint, which will quickly wipe clean, and can be repainted quite easily if it begins to mark too much. This also adds to the impression that the range, drawers, shelves, and cabinets are all part of one large piece of furniture. While the range/dresser is very geometric, an elegant citrus-green armoire adds a touch of swirling fantasy, evoking the fairy tales of Middle Europe with a dash of French chateau style. Based on a cabinet design seen in a baroque German library, and simplified to make it modern, it is a freestanding piece housing the fridge, microwave, and food cabinets. Adding an unexpected touch of romance to a working kitchen/dining room is a good way to lift the atmosphere out of the humdrum.

The sink, along with another run of cabinets, overlooks the garden, and here the emphasis is on simple lines, with drawers of different sizes so that items can be put away and located easily. It is all too easy to have two or three drawers housing a mishmash of kitchen paraphernalia, while seven or eight smaller drawer each with their own few items, are much quicker and easier use. A dishwasher is concealed beside the sink, indistinguishab from the other drawers and cabinets, and the whole area painted in soft lilac. The beech countertop is edged with stainle steel – cleverly combining traditional and modern materials.

Another "dresser" runs along the fourth wall, and here slatte doors, each with carved hearts and the initial of a member of t family, continue the European fairy-tale feel in understate contemporary lines. There is little extraneous detail, but wh there is makes each piece of furniture or run of cabinets ju slightly different from the next, an essential element in t "country" look.

The floor has been painted with a hard-wearing, cream pai through which the wood grain shows. It can be cleaned in t same way as vinyl or linoleum. The color scheme, a mix of lila turquoise, and green with vivid pink, required experimentation get the right shades. With so much color, details were kept plai This has kept the look clean, yet warm and family-friendly.

1: The shallow, wide drawers of the "map" chest unit make it easy to find everything that is stored in there.

2: All the necessary kitchen equipment is neatly hidden from view in built-in or freestanding cabinets.

3: The striking "armoire" cupboard was inspired by the style of a baroque cabinet in a German library.

right: Custom-designed storage means making special shelves f cereals and mounting narrow ones on the doors.

THE COUNTRY KITCHEN/DINING ROOM CHECKLIST

■ Pay close attention to architectural details. Cities can be the same the world over, but country homes usually have a strong sense of age and place. Brickwork, windows, tiles, and fittings, for example, should be appropriate to local traditions rather than following current fashions. If previous owners have "modernized" period or local detail, you may have to spend time researching it, but it will be worthwhile.

■ Mixing, rather than matching, is the essence of a relaxed country kitchen. Instead of following a unified style in the room, try a few different design elements or several colors. Beware of getting too complicated – simple shapes, colors and patterns are easier to juxtapose and more in keeping with a domestic country look.

■ There's no need to keep everything hidden away, but make sure there is a place for everything – preferably easy to reach – or your room will look cluttered. Open shelves and hanging rails will always look right in a cottage setting, but too much can overwhelm.

color

clock

colorful china

range

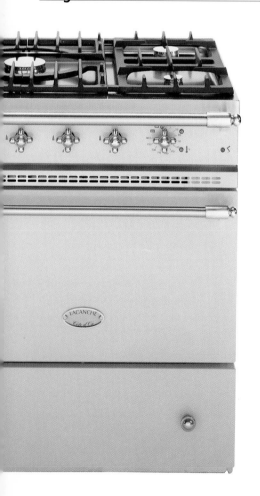

China can be neutral or brightly colored. Matched sets are no longer essential, although an approximate theme will draw a kitchen together. Steel ranges are both traditional and in keeping with contemporary decorative schemes, part of the strong direction toward professional equipment in the kitchen.

modern refectory table

eautiful bowls

electric kettles

the dresser

Wooden furniture, such as dressers and tables, suggests a warm living-room feel, and even essentials, such as pans and kettles, can be chosen for their decorative aspects as well as functional purposes. A combination of high tech and traditional can look very good, especially if both elements are simple.

itchen stools

striped rugs

wooden storage boxes

glassware

A kitchen-living area combines hard and soft textures: glass with wool, wood with cotton, steel with linen. This can work in decorative counterpoint, especially if it doesn't become too complicated. Wood, glass, metal, and ceramics are softened by woven fabrics, but their textures, left unadorned, also speak for themselves.

hanging storage

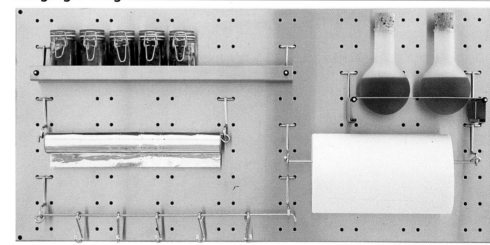

endant lighting

curtain rods

raditional storage

Eating in the kitchen makes everyday flatware, china, and glassware essential to the look. Lighting is critical, and should be on separate circuits – good task lighting over the kitchen zone, elegant pendant lighting or candles for the table, lamps in the living area.

colorful glasses

flatware

OPEN-PLAN

LIVING

An open-plan home is the ultimate in multi-functional living, making the optimum use of space and light. Lack of privacy and noise are sometimes an issue, but, ironically, both very large and very small homes make work best with an open-plan or virtually open-plan layout. Apartments carved out of industrial buildings, such as warehouses, make stunning open-plan spaces, and can be difficult to divide into conventional rooms anyway. At the other end of the spectrum, a living space made of two, three or four boxlike and unattractive rooms can be transformed by knocking down walls and rolling all the functions into one.

It is important to employ a qualified surveyor, builder or architect to ensure that load-bearing walls are properly supported by extra joists, and make sure that the room, especially the storage, is fully planned before starting work. Built-in furniture makes the best use of space, but mistakes are difficult to rectify afterwards.

large space/ loft living

"Loft" or warehouse apartments are the epitome of stylish living today, and this multi-purpose living space in a converted warehouse shows that such homes are not just for young single people. This spacious room can be used for relaxing, dining, working, as a children's play zone, and for business presentations. The secret is to have just a few big pieces of furniture that can easily be moved, plus good storage with a walk-in closet situated just off the main room.

A restrained use of color works well in a multi-functional space – these blue sofas make a bold statement against the neutral shades. The white china and clear glass collection in the kitchen, seen from the main room, does not intrude.

the brief

This family is quite typical of today. One, and sometimes both, partners work full-time from home. Their business activities include design work, building prototypes, administration, and presentations. Children from a previous marriage also live here part of the time. The whole family enjoys socializing, and the space, although generous, is used to full capacity. At the weekend and during the evening the room is used mainly as a play area or for entertaining, while during the day it is often wholly taken over with business activities. Switching from one activity to another takes the minimum of time, as toys, games, and meals can be put away and audiovisual equipment, drawing boards, and papers can be pulled out. The sofas can be used either for informal meetings or for watching television, and a long table can host either a dinner party or a meeting for 12 people. And the

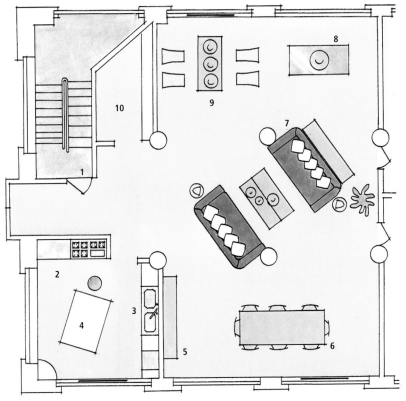

above: To keep the feeling of the room light and airy, these cabinets have been mounted on the partition wall, rather than standing on the floor. The rectangular shape of each cabinet mirrors the lines of the partition, creating a pleasing sense of simplicity and style.

FLOORPLAN

(1) From the stairs and entrance area the kitchen is easily reached (2). There is one short working zone of sink and surfaces (3), and ultra-flexible storage/work surface is achieved with a central roll-around unit (4). Dining room storage cabinets are hung on the partition half-wall (5), and the dining table is conveniently close (6). There is a central "living" zone (7), a table for working (8), and a small conference area (9). Keeping multi-functional space free from clutter is essential, so a large walk-in closet (10) has been built.

above right: The view from the kitchen to the living area.

1: Finding the right size of furniture for an unconventional room can be difficult. Here two standard coffee tables have been placed side by side to make one larger piece.

2: Glass shelves in front of a window allow light to flood in but also create storage space.

3: The island storage cabinetry with countertop is on wheels.

4: A steel-fronted refrigerator and steel range make a stylish, practical kitchen.

enormous amount of china, glass, and other items is stored in a mixture of wall cabinets and open shelves, with a good run of built-in cabinets in a closet off the main room, plus a sizable walk-in closet.

partitions

Even open-plan spaces require some division between areas. Partitions can be built-in or flexible, and can range from whole or half walls to curtains, blinds, screens, and storage units. Even furniture can act as a demarcation line, or a simple change in color or pattern can denote a different usage of the area. Partitions should perhaps be seen as incomplete walls that do not cut out the light but which can have some furniture hung or placed against them.

When deciding how many partitions you will need, and where they should be, list your priorities. Do you need to conceal activities, such as cooking and washing the dishes, or to let in light? Do you need more storage in the room? Partitions are usually excellent sites for cabinets. And how much space do you need on either side of the partition? In this apartment, the owners opted for a shoulder-height wall between the kitchen and living area to allow the maximum light to come in from the windows and to give the opportunity for the cook to chat to those in the living area. Yet at that height, it also offers complete concealment of cooking activities — piles of dirty dishes can be safely left on the kitchen side without making the main room look untidy or at all cluttered.

the kitchen

As most restaurant kitchens prove, a perfect kitchen doesn't have to be big, but you do need to look at how you live, and how you want to use the kitchen, before planning it, rather than simply installing as many cabinets as you can fit into the space.

The first thing to establish is the location of the kitchen area. Ideally, it should be easily reached from the outside door, so that shopping can be unloaded as quickly and easily as possible. It also needs to give good access to the dining room or eating area, as it is tedious to carry plates and dishes any distance. If you look at the floor plan on the previous page, you'll see that the location of this kitchen area fulfills these two criteria.

Second, try to keep the cooking and preparation area as compact as possible so that you don't constantly need to walk in between them every time you cook a meal. The fashion for having as much countertop as possible has now been replaced by identifying activities: a wet area, a chopping area, and a serving area. Then work out the minimum space you will need to operate efficiently in each zone. And as food is usually prepared and chopped before it is served, you may be able to combine these two zones. This kitchen has only one run of cabinets along the partition wall, where the chopping area and sink are located, but has additional work surface cum storage space on top of a roll-around central set of six cabinets bolted together on wheels. This offers more room for food preparation and a big zone which can be used as a serving area. These six units are like a far bigger version of the popular roll-around butcher's block, with hospital-

bed-style wheels, which lock it into position. The wheels ca[n] easily be unlocked so that the whole unit can be pushed against [a] side wall when necessary to free up more floor space.

It is also worth looking at how additional storage has bee[n] added in this kitchen. As the kitchen is placed on a corner it ha[s] only one wall, and that is completely occupied by the stove an[d] fridge. There is a small space for open corner shelves between th[e] two windows, but in order to create more storge space, th[e] owners have built glass shelves over the window, and used the[m] for storing glass. This achieves a maximum storage area witho[ut] cutting out light, although having all the glassware on ope[n] shelves does mean that it needs dusting or washing mo[re] frequently than it would if it was in protected cabinets.

the living zone

A long table is situated at the heart of this apartment. It is adjace[nt] to the kitchen area — the most sensible place to put it — and it [is] used for daily meals, working, and entertaining. In a big spac[e] large pieces of furniture are the most flexible. If a desk and [a] smaller dining table had been placed together they would hav[e] looked more cluttered and been less adaptable.

Large-scale furniture not only looks generous, but it [is] comfortable to live with. Big pieces also match the scale of th[e] room, while lots of smaller items might give the impression of [a] big area with very little in it. Huge sofas are indulgent when the[re] are only one or two people are using them, but can be ver[y] sociable when more people are being entertained.

Big furniture can also be the central part of a color scheme. I[n] an open-plan space there are relatively few walls to paint, so th[e] atmosphere will be created by the color and shape of th[e] furnishings. Here two large blue sofas act as a focal point in th[e] room, but finding a coffee table that was large enough to loo[k] good proved to be a problem. The solution was to buy two [of] them and place them side-by-side. This is a trick that can easily b[e] adapted to other pieces of furniture, such as chests of drawers o[r] bookcases, if you can't find ones that are big enough to suit th[e] overall scale of the room.

LARGE SPACE/LOFT LIVING CHECKLIST

■ Think big in furniture, fixtures and finishes. Standard furniture and conventional patterns could look like doll's furniture next to high ceilings and exposed brickwork.

■ Industrial buildings are usually wide and can lose too much light with conventional rooms and corridors. Partitions – almost to the ceiling or half-height – can provide privacy while allowing light through.

■ Look for bargains. Extra space means you can use industrial or catering-size equipment, such as sinks or ranges, which you can buy relatively inexpensively at auctions. Big secondhand furniture can also go cheaply.

■ Remember that workmen may not be used to converting industrial buildings, so if you are told you "can't have" something, check elsewhere. Dealers and builders may be learning as much as you are.

■ Flooring and countertops can be expensive over large areas, so check out cheaper materials, such as plywood and concrete, which can be painted, sealed, or varnished.

small space/ studio

Four tiny dark rooms have been transformed into a stylish, open-plan studio by architect Jason Cooper, who removed all the internal walls and raised half the floor area. A bath is sunk under a sliding bed, storage space is created on the walls, in steps, and under the floor, and even an office is incorporated. This space is a comprehensive blueprint of good ideas to suit small-space living.

A simple white scheme and honey-colored wood maximize light and space in this small room. Much of the decoration is from architectural detail, such as the bookcases in the dividing wall. Leaving the backsplash painted, not tiled, in the kitchen brings it visually into the living area.

a total living zone

This studio apartment formerly consisted of four dark, high, narrow rooms. When architect Jason Cooper knocked down all the walls, this allowed light to flood from front to back. Although still small overall, he has created a totally flexible space for socializing, working, cooking, eating, and bathing. Everything except the toilet is in the one room. There is an L-shaped kitchen area against the wall, a sofa and table next to it in the "living" space, with steps up to the raised back area, which has a bed, a bath, and an office. This bed area is not immediately visible from the living quarters because a half-height wall, with a bookcase on one side and the office desk on the other, partially screens it without obstructing the light. The *pièce-de-résistance* is the bed, which slides smoothly to one side to reveal a sunken bath underneath. The only separate room is the area in the hallway outside, under the stairs, which houses a toilet. A washing machine has also been squeezed into this space. Everything is painted white. This works well in a small, busy space as it will wear more quickly than in a bigger room, and white paint can be easily retouched.

above: The sofa with the bookcase behind. On the other side of the bookcase is the desk area, concealed by the height of the bookcase.

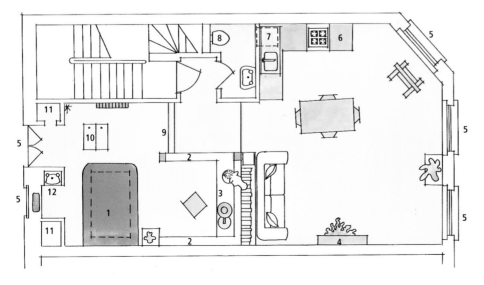

FLOORPLAN
(1) Bed with bath underneath. (2) Bookshelves. (3) Desk. (4) Fireplace. (5) Windows. (6) Kitchen cabinets. (7) Draining board with washing machine underneath (facing toilet area). (8) Toilet in separate room, facing washing-machine door. (9) Drawers fitted into steps. (10) Hatch to underfloor storage. (11) Cupboards on either side of windows. (12) Basin turned sideways between windows.

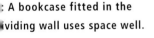

A bookcase fitted in the dividing wall uses space well.

This cupboard under the stairs houses the toilet (not seen) and, facing it, a washing machine, sited in space carved from the "L" of the kitchen.

Large, flat drawers have been fitted into the stair treads. Here they hold artworks, but they could easily store flatware, stationery, or other items.

above and right: Horizontal "lines" are everywhere, achieved by the raised floor, lengths of bookcases, rattan blinds, and the rectangular shape created by the dividing wall, making a narrow space seem wider. This device is carried through to the kitchen, with long cabinet handles, and by painting the kick-board white at the base, the lines "float" horizontally on the wall. A removable metal strip makes a neat junction between the wall and countertop.

■ Plan before buying – list all activities, such as entertaining, eating, cooking, watching television, and working. Draw a scale plan of your apartment, identifying zones for each. Change it around to see if it works better.

■ List all storage requirements before you build or furnish. Don't forget clothes, books, large items, such as suitcases, cooking, and eating utensils, cleaning materials, towels, office and sports equipment.

■ Measure before buying furniture. Can you save space by building in, for example, bench seating with storage beneath it or a platform bed with a desk below?

■ Think vertically. Cut down on furniture by using the walls for lights, shelving, peg rails, hanging cupboards and nightstands (shelves).

■ Cupboard frames and doors use up more space than open shelves. Vary heights of shelves to maximize storage.

■ Think big. One large sofa will be more comfortable and take up less space than two small pieces of furniture.

sleeping, bathing, and working

Living in this studio never feels cramped because when the bath is in use it feels like being in a giant bathroom, at night it is a huge bedroom, and when the owner works at the desk, it is a spacious home office. These three functions interlock, however, because the bed slides into the office when the bath is in use.

First, the bed, as well as being on runners, has drawers for storage built in its base, so that no chest of drawers is needed. Neither are nightstands required, because small shelves with space for a book, a glass of water, and a clock have been set on the wall on either side, carefully positioned so that the bed can

above: The bath ready for use, with the bed sliding back toward the desk area.

1: This basin, mirror, and cupboard are built into the area between two windows. Placing the basin sideways, not into the room, conceals it from view.

2: Cupboards have been built around the windows, making them look deep-set. Blinds are space-saving and practical, and reinforce the "horizontal" theme.

3: A hatch in the floor opens up to store suitcases and large objects. The space was created out of the raised floor.

4: The office area. The desk is set below the top of the dividing half-wall to conceal papers and books from the living area. It also prevents things from falling off the desk and onto the sofa on the other side.

slide beneath them. The reading lights are also set into the wall. All these tricks would be useful in any small bedroom – even if you don't want to go as far as fitting a bath under your bed, you can create a big storage area under the floor in the same way. There is always some space between the floor and the ceiling below, but more depth has been created by building up the floor. This achieved several objectives. First, it helped delineate the different living zones. Second, because the ceilings are quite high for such a narrow space, a higher floor improved the perspective, making the room seem wider and more horizontal. Third, it gave more space under the floor for bulky storage: there are hatches set almost invisibly into the pine planks.

More storage has been built around the windows, making them look attractively deepset. A washbasin over a small cupboard has been inset into the side of the pillar that sits between the windows, and two cabinets are on either side, one housing the boiler and the other a small wardrobe. Everything, has been built in, making full use of vertical space on walls and under the floor.

In the office area there is a desk, with a two-drawer file cabinet beneath it, and several sets of bookshelves. As well as the bookshelves along one wall, there are also shelves set into the dividing half-walls. Not only for storage these shelves form a useful barrier between the sleeping and living areas.

cooking, eating, and living

There's no distinction between food preparation, eating, and living areas because there simply isn't the space. This means that, when it's not in use, the kitchen needs to look as much like living room furniture as possible. The solution was a set of contemporary beech cabinets, plus a beech countertop to echo the floorboards. The shape was laid out to reinforce the horizontal lines in the rest of the space with long, thin door handles and a kickboard painted to match the walls.

The living area has been kept deliberately empty to make the room feel bigger. The table provides an extra work surface, and there is a huge sofa against the dividing half-wall, but, apart from a television table, there is virtually no other furniture.

color

flexible furniture

curving lines

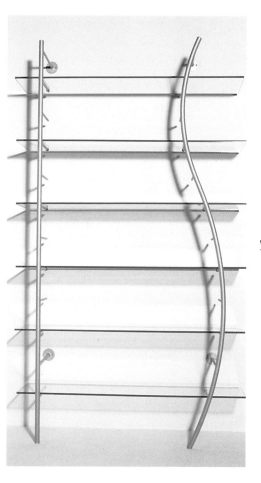

Open-plan living requires a degree of flexibility in furnishings, even in large spaces, as static room layouts are rarely possible. Tables, chests, or sofas that slot together, extending or contracting according to requirements, and shelving or storage acting as room dividers all work well.

contemporary shelving

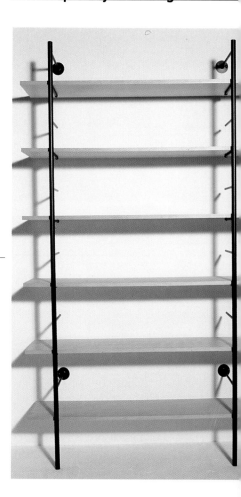

wall lights

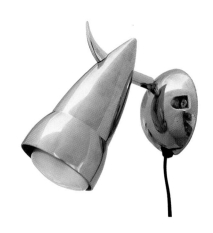

extendable tables

coffee table on wheels

kit furniture

Furniture on wheels, collapsible or kit furniture, and extendable tables all offer a range of options for open-plan living. Scale is important – large rooms need bigger fittings, although smaller studios can also benefit from one or more outsize pieces to prevent a dollhouse effect.

radiators in all colors

modular seating

roll-around furniture

Some furniture is designed with pieces that can extend indefinitely for large rooms, but sometimes the principle can be adapted for ordinary furniture. Shapes can be varied according to how the room is used, especially when items are wheeled, stackable, or lightweight.

tables that slot together

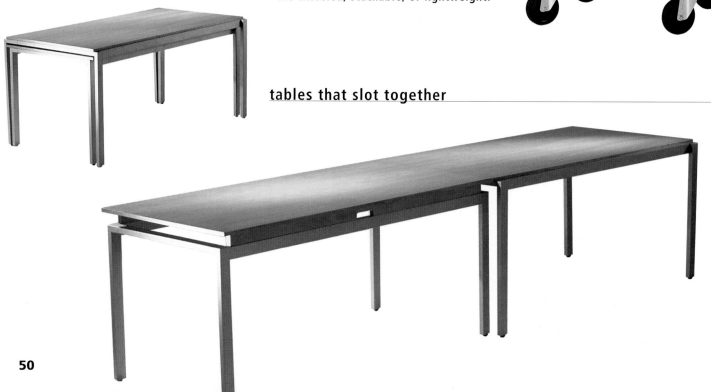

vertical storage racks

vibrant colors and patterns

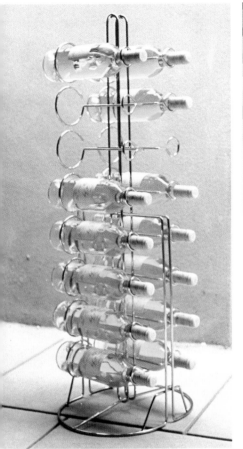

classic shapes

Use vertical space in open-plan living, either to make the most of small studios or to add proportion to larger areas. Ceiling or wall racks or free-standing stacks and racks can all offer surprisingly generous storage facilities. Hooks, peg rails, and shelving also make the most of wall space.

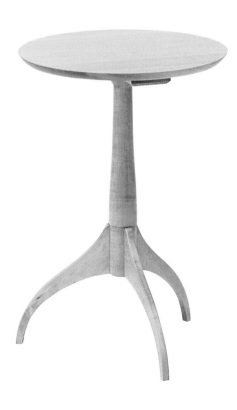

stackable seating

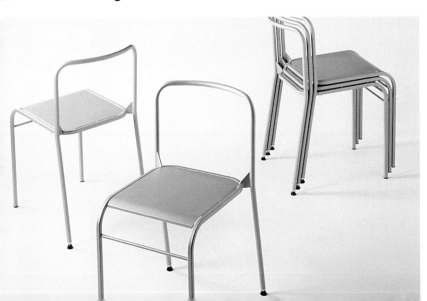

LIVING AND

WORKING

Working from home is a growing trend, as advances in telecommunications free people from daily commuting, but this places pressure on space. Dual-purpose rooms are the answer, with good storage so that you can switch the room from one function to another with ease.

When deciding which room to use, assess your lifestyle. Who else lives in the house? No-one can work whilst in charge of babies or toddlers, so a door that shuts is essential. Other adults may feel excluded if your office dominates the main room, or if they have to adapt their lives around your work. And do you have enough privacy? If you find open-plan offices distracting, there is no point duplicating the situation at home.

Above all, there is a major difference between being a self-employed person and running a business which involves other people from home. If colleagues and clients are frequently in the house, your family life may well be affected.

the home office/ dining room

This is a dining room that can seat eight people at a round table in the evening, and during the day it becomes a home office. The tall, narrow custom-built cabinets in each corner open up to reveal a computer, printer, files, and box storage. The "desk" is a pull-out bureau-style flap below the computer, and the central table provides extra space at one side on which to place papers and documents.

Two identical cabinets were custom-built to provide a home office and dining room storage. A central section pulls out like a bureau top, revealing a slot for a laptop or small computer. Cupboards above and below house the printer, computer systems unit, and files. The matching cabinet has space to store glasses, plates, and flatware.

■ Dining room chairs should only be used briefly. Otherwise use a stable office chair that is height- and back-adjustable, with casters and a swivel action. Armrests should also be adjustable.

■ You should work facing your computer, never twisted to the side. Feet should be flat on the floor or on a footrest, with your eyebrows in line with the top of the screen, elbows at your sides and forearms parallel to the floor.

■ Do you have enough outlets? When concealing equipment, drill holes for cords at the back of shelves or cabinets, and ensure air-holes if doors are left closed – electrical equipment gets hot!

■ To calculate storage, list the items you use daily over a week, for example magazines, pens, stationery, and books. If you use them often, they should be easy to reach. Boxes, baskets, and drawer dividers insure that space is used effectively.

■ A hands-free option prevents neck-strain if you use the phone regularly.

the brief

This room has three functions – it is the main entrance hall of the house, it acts as a formal dining room for dinner parties, and it is a home office for a busy stylist and working mother. Mail is left on the table in the morning, then the right-hand cabinet is opened up to reveal a computer, filing system, and printer, so that any correspondence can be answered, sorted, and filed. Letters and documents are written on the computer, and swatches and invoices are stored on the shelves. This home office is essentially an administrative center, used only for a few hours a day, so it needs less storage than a full-time business would. When work finishes, only a few moments are needed to pack papers away in their files, fold up the bureau flap, and close the cupboard doors before laying the table for a dinner party. This doesn't happen every day, as most family meals are eaten upstairs in the kitchen-dining room, but the office element is compact enough, and also sufficiently well organized, to switch from one function to the other with the minimum of fuss.

the furniture

For most people, concealing the computer and its associated equipment is the key to a successful dual-purpose room. There is an increasing number of home office cabinets on the market, but for this dining room/office, the owners had furniture specially commissioned. Here two tall, narrow cabinets, one with a pull-out desk and computer inside, and the other with mixed office and dining room storage, have been commissioned to stand in each corner of a small square dining room. A circular table makes the most of the central space for dining, seating eight people. During the day the same table can be used for meetings or as extra work space when there is a lot of paperwork.

Commissioning furniture need not be costly, and often offers good value for money. The cupboards here are made of inexpensive MDF (medium density fiberboard), and having them made insured that they fit exactly into the space. The stylish

1

2

1: A roll-around file can be wheeled out of sight.

2: Document boxes use vertical space well and contain miscellaneous paperwork.

Above: The dining table functions as an extra work area and it can also hold client meetings and host dinner parties. The soft lilac walls work for day or evening.

The blinds at the windows lend a clean, professional look. They are also effective at filtering sunlight from the computer screen, and take up less space than drapes.

handles help dispel any "office" feel, and the tall, thin shape utilizes vertical space, freeing up floor area for the large, round table. Had the owners adopted the more conventional layout of a desk-high run of cabinets along the wall, there would have been less room to place the table and chairs, and the "office" look would have been much more noticeable.

Furniture makers or carpenters can be found at all price levels, although it will always be more expensive than buying from the very cheapest mass-market shops. Ask around locally for recommendations – word of mouth is always an effective way of insuring good workmanship. When commissioning a carpenter or furniture maker, ask to see pieces of previous work or to look at a portfolio of past work. When discussing what you want, be as precise as you can, and write the brief down. It should include all the functions you will need from the piece of furniture and the equipment you want to house. If you have any photographs from magazines showing the style you like, attach them. If someone is producing original designs, indicate what your own tastes are, for example, contemporary, traditional, Shaker, or classic. Always ask to see preliminary sketches, and carefully check such measurements as heights of the computer screen and keyboard, the range of any opening doors, and the space allowed for yourself. Never assume that the craftsman knows what is in your mind, and make sure you understand exactly what is planned, and the price that is agreed, before giving the final go-ahead. When the piece is delivered, check the stability and strength, especially hinges and joints, before making the final payment. Finally, do understand that commissioning work is not an instant process – a desk may be delivered from a shop in ten days, but it may take weeks or months to complete a piece of furniture from scratch. However, the result will usually be ten times more satisfying, and in the case of difficult dual-purpose situations, it may be your only option.

lighting

The type of lighting needed is critical in both an office and a dining room, which have directly opposing requirements. An office needs good overall light plus task lighting, such as a adjustable desk lamp (not a conventional table lamp, which give a glow rather than a practical directional beam). Compute screens should be shielded from glare. A dining room, in contras works best with low, intimate light and candles. This office-dining room has low-voltage halogen spotlights in the ceiling, which a operated on a dimmer switch to offer bright, daylight-qualit light during work hours, or a warm soft glow in the evening. desk lamp supplies the directional light. You also have to contro the sunlight – it shouldn't reflect into your eyes or onto th computer screen. Blinds, as used here, are usually more effectiv than curtains, and they keep the atmosphere businesslike durin the day. Blinds are also space-saving in a small room, such as th one, so they work well all round.

color

A dual-purpose office-dining room presents a different challeng to a single-use dining room or office. In a dining-room that i mainly used at night, strong or vibrant colors are often used t add warmth, but if the room is also used during the day, this ma not be appropriate. Before choosing a vivid shade or a bus wallpaper do think about whether you can work and live with all day every day. That doesn't mean you have to choose a blan color – the right shade will help to dispel any office gray. A office-dining room has great potential for clutter, so simplicit (using just one or two themes or colors) is usually the best polic Here, one wall has been painted a soft lilac while the other wall are white, and the rest of the furniture is limited to natural woo or metal shades, linking the wood of a dining room with th more high-tech metallics of an office.

To distract the eye even further from any office clutter, a fe splashes of vibrant color – the vivid pinks and purples of th chair seats, and a big bunch of flowers – have also been added t the room. When the owners get bored with the scheme and wan to ring the changes, they can just repaint one wall and change th dining chair seat covers, to end up with the ultimate solution fo flexible living.

Storage

Most offices need a combination of boxes, files, and easily accessible trays and pots. All can now be bought in a wide range of colors, or you can stick to classic neutrals, such as black, beige, gray, or white. They can be concealed behind cupboard doors, or placed on wheels to be rolled aside, or furniture – from entire cupboards to simple blanket boxes – can be bought or adapted to hold them. A good rule of thumb is to work out what you need, but be generous and make sure there is scope for expansion as time goes on.

FLOORPLAN
(1) Table. (2) Custom-built dining and office storage cupboard. (3) Storage cupboard with pull-out desk. (4) Roll-around file cabinet.

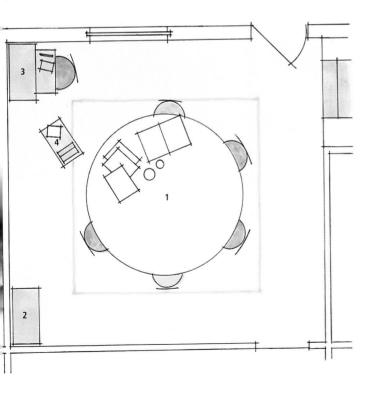

above: Flowers and candles complete the finishing touches of the conversion from office to dining room, and visitors are unlikely to realize that this room is used as an office during the day.

the office/ living room

This large, stunning room is central to both a home and a flourishing business. Designed by architect Gunnar Orefelt, it is more than just a home office, it is a client meeting room, a living room for relaxing, and a dining room for family eating and occasional large parties. To one side is the kitchen and family area and to the other, the main office of a busy architectural practice.

White walls are light and professional, but a living room needs color. Here panels of vivid terra-cotta and blue offer a focal point for the eye and a background for pictures, while the surrounding areas stay neutral. The computer is not concealed, but overshadowed by a contemporary painting.

■ Look ahead five or ten years. Cash flow and flexibility mean you can't always move immediately if the business grows. Build in scope for expansion. And your family situation may change – you may marry or have more children. Plan how to adapt.

■ A separate entrance for colleagues and clients is an important consideration. The office also needs its own basic kitchenette and toilet to preserve family privacy.

■ Insure that the office and home can work independently of each other. A separate building, such as a converted barn, or at least a clear division between home and office means that you can switch off more easily.

■ Divide storage into short- and long-term. Think ahead: six years' worth of accounts may need to be stored in a secure shed or garage, for example. Even short-term storage expands quickly. Double your initial calculations.

■ Plan how you will cope with a rush job, late working or more staff, without taking over the house completely.

a home to a business

This is the headquarters of a busy architect's practice as well as a home, in contrast to the previous office-dining room, which was on a much smaller scale and was a home office for one self-employed person. It is essential to recognize the difference when you are planning to work from home because the demands on space and equipment are completely different, and the need to keep a defining line between your personal life and your work becomes far greater. Don't underestimate how resentful even the most supportive members of your family can become if they feel that their home has been completely invaded by your work, particularly if you have colleagues visiting, employees working there, or long client meetings. It is less difficult if you live with someone who goes out to work themselves, although a sudden rush or a project that requires all-night working can invade their precious private time as well as yours. Anyone who is based at

above: It's hard to tell where family books and videos stop and architectural files begin. Suspending the shelves centrally on the wall helps prevent them looking too dominant, and the radiator underneath echoes the shape

home, such as a mother with young children, or someone working at home in a different profession, may well feel that her home is no longer her own. Either way, it is important to build in as much division between home and the business as possible, and you too will feel the benefit when you want to switch off.

This large room is literally the link between the architect's offices to one side, and the kitchen and bedrooms on the other. Originally it was designed to function as a meeting room and research library for the offices, while being combined with a dining room and living room for the family. As a generous room with a folding table it offered scope for large parties – either professional ones given by the practice or just social occasions. However, as the business expanded, it became necessary to move a desk and workstation into one end of it, and to use some of the family storage for files and papers. Fortunately, the flexible design and the simple fittings mean that this still looks streamlined and stylish, and the two fuse seamlessly into one.

above: The colored panels behind each picture were painted in an afternoon, and could be changed again equally quickly.

1: A few striking pieces of art, such as this painting by Sally Greaves-Lord, are on a large scale to match the room.

2 and 3: The white table folds in triangles, so that it can be used for either big client meetings or dinner parties.

4: Many books are stored on the shelves. The rolled drawings are due for long-term storage.

furniture and fittings

The furnishings for a business run from home have to be much more hard-wearing than those for a home or even a home office, and this has an impact on everything you buy, from flooring and paintwork to chairs and tables. This is mainly because a business generates more people. For example, a meeting with more than six colleagues could happen twice a week, whereas few homeowners would have a dinner party for that number so often. People also treat a business area differently, not out of bad manners but because they're concentrating on work, rather than their environment. So they are likely to do things such as leaning back on the chairs to make a point at a meeting, walking in with dirt on their shoes, and so on. It may not sound as if it makes that much difference, but architect Gunnar Orefelt estimates that the wear and tear on company furniture and fittings is about four times as much as that on home furnishings. This doesn't mean

FLOOR PLAN
(1) Desk and computer.
(2) Extendable dining and meeting table. (3) Long shelving for books and documents. (4) Living zone.
(5) Decorative panels of vivid color.

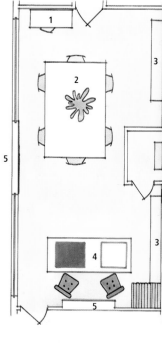

right: Look at contemporary styles to find well-designed, hard-wearing contract furniture, but that doesn't mean that your home has to be entirely modern in feel. Here chairs by Scandinavian designer Bruno Mathsson sit happily side-by-side with a traditional oil portrait.
far right: Splashes of color, such as a vase of bright flowers, distract the eye from office equipment.

ou have to buy office furniture, but it is worth checking out ompanies that supply both homes and offices, and discussing ow well the furniture is built to wear before buying it. Today's ovement toward contemporary furniture is an enormous help, ecause you are more likely to find well-designed contract rniture that will also look good in a home environment. Think out how the furniture will look at the meeting as well as in the ning room; for example, some kitchen chairs may not look rofessional enough for a meeting. On the other hand, elegant bric-covered dining room chairs may not last well. The table, o, should be of a flexible size and finish so that you don't worry out any surface stains when you are working.

Flooring is another key issue. Here the floor is a hard-wearing ech, but there are many cheaper versions on the market, some which will not stand up to extensive wear. Wooden floors will ed resanding and varnishing every few years, so if you buy a veneered wooden floor, check the depth of veneer and how often you will be able to restore it. There is a huge choice of contract flooring, ranging from sisal and seagrass floor coverings to plain and patterned carpeting intended for hotels, linoleum (which can be laid in any pattern you like), and tiled, rubber, and vinyl floorings. You should be able to achieve almost any effect you like, but do check that it is suitable for heavy use.

You will probably even need to re-paint more often, especially if you want to give a smart impression to clients. This makes wallpaper a less suitable option, and may limit your color scheme to something simple and easily matched, such as white, which can be used to touch up one wall or a heavy-duty area without worrying about matching up tones. You can enliven the look by painting one wall or a panel in a different color. Here panels of vivid color are used to add vibrancy to an all-white scheme, but they could be painted over in an afternoon.

left: A raised floor level denotes a casual seating area, and the "living-room" end of the spacious room.

65

the bedroom/ study

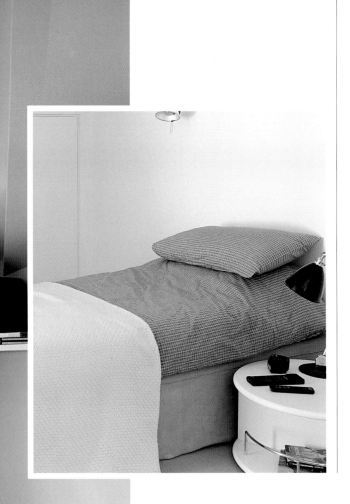

This bedroom-study was carved out of the roof to give a teenage boy his own room. Although the house's floor area was generous, the roof slopes steeply, so architect Barbara Weiss had restricted space within which to work. The most important element in the study is the built-in storage, which runs virtually all around the room. It is so extensive that there is no need for any furniture other than a bed and built-in desk area. Leftover cabinet space is used by the family for long-term storage.

Everything in this bedroom-study is built in: there is a niche for the TV and VCR, with pull-out drawers beneath for videos. Different-size **cabinets in the room store clothes and larger items such as suitcases. The bed (inset) can easily be moved around the room.**

room for growth

Sleeping and working in the same room is not ideal, but it is often the only option for students who have exams looming. Here the extensive and carefully planned storage means that everything can be tidied away easily, to keep the two worlds separate. Nothing is more distracting than being unable to find your notes because they're lost among your clothes. The rooms of children and teenagers are often the smallest or most awkwardly shaped in a house, and this is when it is usually more efficient to build all storage in, rather than place bookcases and chests of drawers against a sloping wall.

This kind of storage needs to be thought out before the first shelf is cut. Each shelf and drawer will have to be custom-made to fit its slot, as the variable shapes and sizes mean you don't have the option of adjustable shelving. Drawers can be varied in size: drawers divided into sections will keep CDs and videos tidy and easy to see, while bigger drawers can take bulkier things. Don't decide on the size of the drawers and shelves without measuring what has to go inside – you'll just waste space and even find yourself with drawers that can't be used for much. Shallow drawers can take pens and pencils, makeup and miscellaneous small items, medium-size drawers are suitable for clothes, videos, CDs, and books, while larger ones can ta. sweaters, bedding, and so on. Small, but deep cabinets can ta suitcases. Full-length hanging space is likely to be scarce in such room, so work out where it can fit first and build the rest of th storage around it. A TV, VCR, and other electronic equipment c. be built into open shelves – just plan the wiring so that it is o of sight. A sizable desk can be built cheaply by cutting a lar piece of wood to rest on two filing cabinets or chests of drawers

This cabinetry almost disappears and becomes part of the w. because all the decorative detail on it has been kept to minimum, and it has been painted the same brilliant white as t rest of the room to offset the room's smallness.

total storage solutions

Many people look at their roof to see if they can expand upward especially as older children need somewhere they can enterta and work, rather than just sleep and play. Often this is an excelle solution. However, it is not necessarily simple. In many place there are limitations on what can be done in the houses, and t importance of maintaining "the roofline" is something that growing increasingly crucial in many cities. Nevertheless, it

1: A roller shade protects the dormer window from glare.

2: Wall lighting saves space and means no side tables are needed.

3: A structured office chair proves you can be ergonomic and stylish.

far right: The built-in desk has been planned to maximize the width of the window area.

■ Make sure the attic room will satisfy any restrictive covenants that may be in force.

■ Employ an architect to make maximum use of a difficult space.

■ The position of windows can be critical. Roof windows or skylights may provide more light than dormer windows. Set at the right angle, they provide light equally to all areas of the room. Many shapes are available, as well as custom-made versions.

■ Even if the attic covers the entire floor area of the house, a pitched roof will mean that only a percentage of the space is made available.

■ Insulation and ventilation are critical, so don't be tempted to skimp on them.

■ The size and tread height of the stairs may be governed by regulations, so stairways may take up much more space than you had planned. You should not use just a ladder.

■ With a pitched roof it is more effective to build in storage, rather than trying to fit free standing furniture.

often possible to convert the attice into a room without altering the framework of the building, with small dormer windows, skylights, or roof windows that are scarcely noticeable. In any area where restrictive covenants apply, you need to insure that any exterior alterations will fit in with your building's style. It is worth noting that you will not necessarily be allowed to bypass a covenant prohibiting alterations to the roof just because a neighbor has – controls are often tight.

Then consider restrictions inside. First, with sloping roofs, you can only stand in a small area. Legislation on the room's height is usually in force and any alterations will have to meet these.

Second, you will have to give up space on the landing below, or possibly even give up a small room, to make a staircase. Where and how you erect the stairs may also be subject to building controls that will restrict the size of tread, the stairs' angle, and the head height in any one place. Staircases must be permanent – an attic room cannot have just a ladder.

Third, you will have to improve the heating and ventilation, as most roof areas are cold in winter and hot in summer. This should help the whole house, as less heat will escape through the roof with better insulation. Even if your window size is restricted by building controls, it may be possible to replace a roof section with toughened conservatory glass that will make good use of overhead light. Skylights can also be better for light than dormer windows.

1: A shelf neatly tucks under the eaves to hold all the teenager's CDs.

2: A table on wheels can be moved easily around the room if necessary.

right: The movable bed is the only major piece of furniture that is situated in the room.

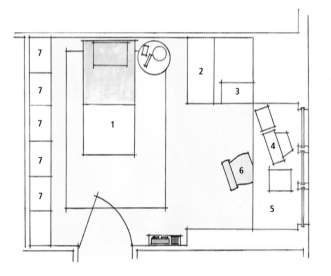

FLOORPLAN
(1) Bed. (2) Built-in storage for TV and VCR. (3) Cupboard under eaves. (4) Computer. (5) Desk. (6) Chair. (7) Built-in cabinetry under eaves.

Carefully planned, built-in
shelving has created a neat
niche to store both the TV
and VCR.

Plenty of light floods into
the bedroom/study from a
glass roof that is over
the hallway.

color

pencil holder

sisal storage baskets

dynamic shapes in cabinets

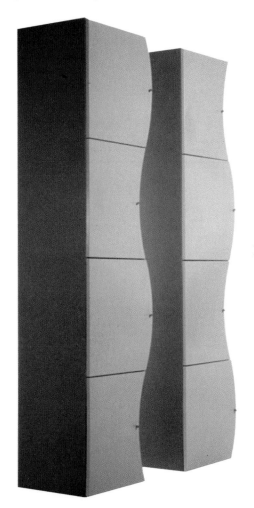

decorative touches

Create your own ideal storage system by collecting and adapting these basics. Boxes and baskets provide essential storage, and file cabinets can work as both storage and room dividers. Measure books, files, and boxes when building customized shelves, and stack the most frequently used items closest to hand.

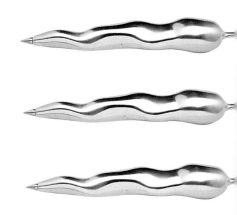

flexible furniture

orizontal drawer handles

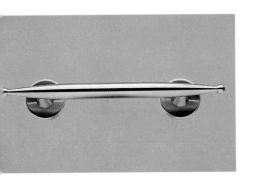

storage drawers

pocket calculators

urved file cabinets

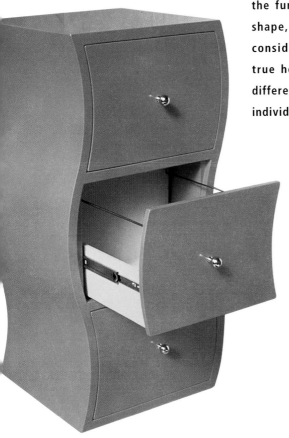

compact seating

The design of workspace furniture should be of as high a standard as the furniture that surrounds it. Color, shape, style, function, and ergonomic considerations all work together in a true home office. Add detail, such as different door and cabinet handles, for individuality.

flexible desk lighting

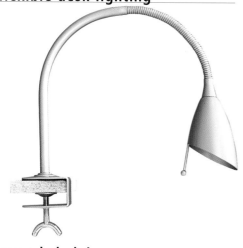

extendable lighting

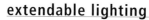

curved shelving

bulletin boards

Task lighting is essential in any work zone. Mount it on the desk or wall to free up space and insure direct light where it's needed most. Bulletin boards serve as instant aide-memoires and provide a quick way of storing lists, notes, or useful addresses. Tables and desks should be expansive and comfortable.

table-cum-desk with drawers

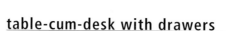

ergonomic seating

roll-around file cabinets

adjustable work tables

antique file cabinets

There are beautiful old wooden desks, cabinets, and chairs to be found in antique and junk shops, but always check they are sound, ergonomic, and comfortable. Adjustable furniture and furniture on wheels are both useful in dual-purpose rooms. Studio couches offer a clean-lined alternative to bulky sofa beds.

studio couch

BEDROOM

PLUS

The bedroom is the real comfort zone. We spend up to one-third of our lives there, yet it is a room with contradictory requirements: relaxing yet organized, informal but well-planned, stylish and comfortable. It's an intensely personal place, but it does waste space to leave it unused for two-thirds of the day.

Dual-purpose solutions include bedroom-bathrooms, bedroom-playrooms and bedroom-studies. For many people, an en-suite bathroom is now a must-have, but rather than carving a small, dark box out of a corner, optimize space by having a bath and sink in the bedroom. It retains a room's original proportions and makes it easier to move around, although it is a solution for a master bedroom, not a family bathroom.

The bedroom-study can give teenagers the privilege of having their own space and privacy, and spare rooms can also be used as office spaces, although your own main bedroom will not be a restful choice as an office.

bed/bath: all in one

Here bed and bath are situated in one flowing space, without any division between the two functions. Built-in storage on two walls enhances, rather than detracts from, the room's original proportions. On one side, space for built-in closets has been taken from the adjacent spare bedroom, with doors cut into the wall to open into this room. On the other, built-in cabinets and drawers surround the windows. Clutter can be cleared away, leaving the bed and bath as focal points.

Combining a master bedroom and bathroom can be a perfect solution to making the best use of space for storage in a limited area. The bath's free-standing position means that an antique-style hand-held shower head with a hose that attaches to the bath faucet is the best option.

the brief

This is the master bedroom of a period family home, which had been changed into two rooms – a bedroom and a bathroom – in earlier years. Although the rooms were a reasonable size, they were not large, and once furniture, such as nightstands and built-in cabinets, was added, space had become quite limited. The owners had enjoyed an open-plan bath in their bedroom in an earlier house, and decided to knock down the wall between the two rooms.

Once they had done so, the line of the floorboards showed that they were, in fact, restoring a big, light room to its original proportions, as well as maximizing the existing floor area. Now, instead of facing a tiled wall and listening to the roar of the extractor fan when they have a bath, they can lie in the hot water and relax by watching the changing seasons in the garden through the bedroom windows.

The basic principle of having bathing facilities in yo bedroom is centuries-old. Houses were not built with purpos designed bathrooms until the nineteenth century, and a was stand, or table with a bowl of hot water, was an established sig in bedrooms. Baths were often portable, and placed in front of fire. Even after bathrooms became commonplace, a sink in t bedroom was customary, but now that even quite mode homes are expected to have two, possibly three, bathrooms this dying out. So you could view the bedroom-bathroom as t reintroduction of an old custom. There is one aspect, howeve that even the least inhibited prefer to keep private – the toile Here it is located in a small walled-off corner of the room, wi its own door, near the bath and sink. Some people may prefer conceal it behind a half-wall, but if this is the case take noise in account as well as the sight line.

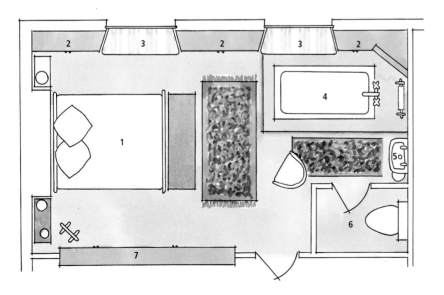

FLOORPLAN
(1) Bed. (2) Built-in cabinets surrounding windows. (3) Window seats with radiators underneath. (4) Bath. (5) Sink. (6) Toilet. (7) Closets using space borrowed from the adjacent room.

1: A separate toilet is normally essential for privacy .

2: The chest at the foot of the bed provides seating and additional storage.

3: This wall of closets was built in the adjacent room, and these are doors that have been cut into the wall.

4: The sink in the corner is a similar Victorian design to the bed and the bath. The wall lights above are sealed in and cannot be reached from the bath.

above: A gentle angle at the window edge of the cabinets allows more light in. Hanging space and drawers break up the cabinetry and suggest paneling. Note how the style of the bath faucet and the bed effectively links them together in a Victorian theme.

the furniture

This room has stylistic unity, which is a key point to remember when combining two functions in one space. The wrought iron bed and Victorian bath and fixtures are essentially both white, and have the same feel to them as they come from a similar era. A modern bath with a Victorian bed, or vice versa, would have been less successful. This doesn't mean that the style has to be Victorian, but it is a reminder that once you have established a style, then it is usually better to stick to it.

The extensive built-in cabinets and drawers insure that the room stays tidy and free of clutter, as the owners made a deliberate decision to create a room that needed very few pieces of furniture in order to maintain the feeling of space. There are only two nightstands and a chest at the end of the bed – even chairs are not needed because of the window seats. This makes the windows, and the view outside, a major decorative feature in the room, drawing the green of the trees inside to blend with the three shades of green in the room.

the practicalities

Water needs a slope to drain away, and one reason why baths are often flush against the wall is that they are closer to the waste pipe in this position. However, you can place a bath in any position in a room. If there is enough space between the floorboards and the ceiling below, the pipes can run below the floor at the correct slant, or, if not, the bath will have to be built on a raised platform as this one is. Very occasionally, people are tempted to add a false ceiling to the room below to accommodate the pipes, but unless the ceiling really is too high, it may interfere with the room's natural proportions. The soil pipe for the toilet is a larger pipe, and, if you propose moving it, you may get protests from your plumber. However, it is almost always possible to move it; it may simply cost more to put it on a platform.

Having an open-plan bedroom-bathroom often means that you can treat yourself to the luxury of a giant bath. What is not apparent here – because it stands in a large area – is that this bath is also exceptionally large, another bonus gained from siting

it centrally in a free-flowing space. The sink, too, is generous proportioned and is in an antique design so that it sits stylish with the bath and bed.

If you have a central bath, remember to include somewhere stand a soap dish or shampoo bottles when you are in the bath This bath is boxed in and this has created a wide enough ri around it for such practicalities, but many freestanding claw-fo baths don't have the kind of edge you could balance a bottle o You will need either to build in a shelf nearby or have a tab standing next to the bath. Similarly, make sure that the towel b is within easy reach – you don't want to walk across the roo dripping with water.

lighting and safety

Careful consideration must be given to lighting and electric equipment anywhere near water, and most countries ha regulations that cover the kind of lamps or sockets that can be used within reach of a bath or sink. Electricity and water ar truly, a lethal combination, and you should never take risk especially when there are children about. While some people bend the rules a bit, it is wise to do so only with the utmost caution. For example, it would be very dangerous indeed to ha any piece of electrical equipment, such as a lamp or a hairdry so near to either the bath or the sink that it might fall in whi would electrocute you. This means that you should not have si tables with lamps or standard lamps anywhere near the bath are In this room the only lighting comes from wall lights, and t lamps are right across the other side of the room on the bedsi tables. Even wall lights should be sealed – there are an increasi number of good bathroom light designs now on the market and you should not be able to change a lightbulb while standi in the bath!

storage

An extensive and well-planned storage system is the key to t serenity of this bedroom. There is a place for everything, a everything is in its place. Two whole walls of storage have be

Cupboard doors open to reveal shelves.

The radiators are below the window seat, allowing the heat to spread out into the room rather than being lost through the window.

Above right: Wooden flooring works well for bathrooms or bedrooms. Vinyls, linoleum, and some carpets are also suitable for a bedroom-bathroom.

designed to fit in unobtrusively without dominating the room. One wall of closets was actually built in the adjacent spare bedroom, with the doors knocked out of the wall between the two rooms and opening into the main bedroom. This involved moving the door to the spare bedroom slightly further along the landing, which was not a difficult job.

The other wall of drawers and cabinets was built around the windows, offering the opportunity for a window seat, and making the windows look attractively deepset. There is a gentle slope at the window edge of each cabinet, making the windows look larger and the window seats more comfortable. The radiators could have posed a problem, but long low ones were installed under the window seats.

BED/BATH: ALL IN ONE CHECKLIST

■ Make sure that no one can use hairdryers or other types of electrical equipment in the bathroom area – it is safer not to site eletrical outlets near the bath or sink. It is also a good idea to use only special bathroom lighting, which fits flush against the wall or ceiling and is sealed. It should never be possible to change a lightbulb when standing in the bath.

■ If you regularly open windows and doors, then you may not wish to use an extractor fan, but it can be useful during the winter months. Bedroom-bathrooms will be bigger than most standard bathrooms so you may need to check with a retailer as to whether you need a more powerful fan.

■ Check that towels are within easy reach, and also that there is a suitable surface near the bath for shampoo bottles, soap, and other accessories.

■ A central bath is not suitable for anything bigger or stronger than a shower head that is hand-held.

the bedroom/ playroom

This bedroom/playroom was designed by James Lynch of City Lofts, London, for a family that has four children, ranging from a small baby to a ten-year-old. By building in a series of different pieces in one coordinated design, he has created a private, lockable desk zone for the eldest child, plus flexible sleeping platforms, lots of storage, a play space, and the option for the area to evolve as the children grow.

A top sleeping platform runs the length of this bedroom/playroom and can take two or three mattresses. Below is a built-in crib, which can convert to a desk area later on. There is also an open playing space that can ultimately house pull-out wardrobes when more storage space is needed, and (inset) a third bed platform.

built-in growth

The starting point for this design was to provide sleeping and playing space for four young children, whose needs will change as they grow up. At first glance, you might expect freestanding furniture to be more flexible than a built-in design, but this series of platform beds, desks, and storage units will adapt to suit their needs and carry them well into their teens.

The flexibility starts with wide sleeping platforms that run the length of the room on either side rather than conventional bunk beds. There is enough space on both sides for extra mattresses to be added if a friend spends the night, and, when the spare

mattress is removed, the platform space can be used for playing. Traditional bunk beds are often quite restrictive, and it can be difficult for an adult to sit up and read to a child. With these platforms there is plenty of room to sit up on both levels, making the extra space useful for board games or model-building – in fact, anything that needs to be kept out of the way of the curious fingers of toddlers or the irritating interference of inquisitive younger children.

The platforms also make better use of the space underneath than ordinary bunk beds. Along one side of the room – where the

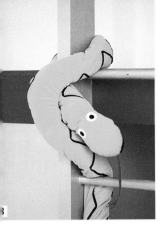

1: The built-in crib has scope to be turned into either a seating area or a second desk zone when the baby grows out of it.

2: The ladder up to the top sleeping platform helps to evoke the era of pirate ships.

3: The bright colors of the room echo the children's toys.

4: Extra storage is slotted in whenever possible.

5: Bulkhead lighting offers individual pools of light.

6: Brightly colored bedlinen adds to the decorative scheme.

eldest child sleeps — there is a long, simple desk-worktop where homework can be done or games can be played. A long sliding door with portholes in it for the light can be slid across and locked, thus keeping this space sacrosanct from the meddling of the younger ones. In this way, the child who has almost reached his teens already is given his own space, while still sharing a room with his brothers and sisters. The desk is one long strip of kitchen countertop — in this case a recycled plastic which is not only cheaper than the equivalent length of wood but also tougher and easier to clean. Underneath the desk surface there is room for file cabinets or more shelving as the need arises, and another chair can be added if two or more children want to work there together. On the other side, where the top platform is longer and will eventually house two mattresses — even three when friends come to stay — the area below is used for a built-in crib, an empty space, and a third, single platform for the toddler, who cannot

FLOOR PLAN
(1) Sleeping platform for oldest child with desk below. (2) Partition to window with holes for light. (3) Window running the width of the room. (4) Extra storage tower. (5) Sleeping platform above built-in crib. (6) Sleeping platform continues over play space. (7) Sleeping platform over lower sleeping platform.

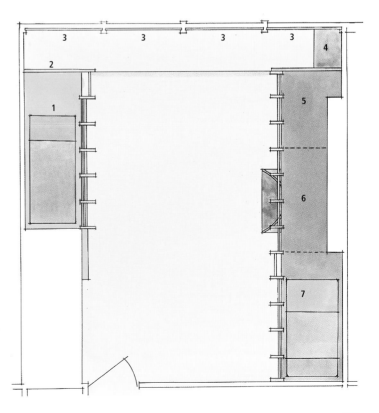

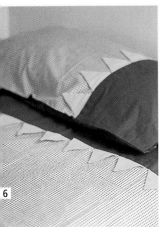

■ Adults protest at children's untidy rooms, yet often fail to provide the storage facilities needed to keep the room tidy. Children's rooms need more comprehensive storage than adults', not less.

■ Don't fob off a child with second-rate furniture, such as drawers that stick or unattractive pieces that have been rejected as sub-standard for the rest of the house.

■ Reassess living and storage needs once a year. The quantity and style of toys and clothes change as children grow up. Think of sports clothes and equipment, hobbies, computers and homework, as well as recreational books.

■ If you start out with a romantic scheme for a small baby, be prepared to redecorate within five years, as he or she may outgrow it.

■Try to provide an extra bed – anything from a trundle bed to a sofa bed. A parent may want to sleep in the same room as a small baby from time to time, and older children enjoy having friends for sleepovers.

safely sleep on top yet. When the baby leaves the crib, the toddler will be old enough to sleep on the upper levels, and the baby will take his position on the lower sleeping platform. Below both the crib and the lower platform, there are pull-out storage boxes set on wheels for toys and clothes, and these will be turned into drawers eventually when the children's toys become less bulky and they need more storage space for clothes.

storage and light

The built-in crib also has storage beneath it and, when the youngest child outgrows it, the rails will be removed, thus eliminating all evidence that it was ever a crib. With the base in its current position, this will turn the area into a little built-in sofa or bench seating. However, there is also the option to raise it to create another desk area, which will be useful in the future when two or even three of the children will have homework or studying to do.

1: One long sleeping platform has room for an extra mattress for a friend, while below is a long desk area with file cabinets.

2: The "porthole" doors slide closed and can be locked.

3: There is plenty of room for books and games on the shelves above and the cabinets below the desk.

The large windows run the whole width of the room, so the [en]d pieces – the equivalent of the foot of a bed – stop just short [of] the windows. Portholes are cut in the left-hand end piece, to [ad]d light to the eldest child's desk area, while the right-hand side [is] used for a tall series of shelves which currently hold more [bo]xes of toys. In future these can also be used as bookcases, [di]splay cases for models, or shelves for storing videos, CDs, and [eq]uipment. The long raised platform at the window acts as either [a] window seat or an extra level for toys and games.

In between the built-in crib and the lowest platform bed is an [em]pty space, which is now used for playing. It gives the children [th]e option of putting up a tent or playing at theater. However, as [th]ey grow up, tents will be less important and storing school [cl]othes and sports equipment will be a problem. The design for [th]e room includes adding three pull-out wardrobes in this area to [in]crease storage. As the depth of the platform is greater than a [w]ardrobe needs to be, the most effective way of maximizing [ha]nging space is to have deep, narrow wardrobes that pull out on [ca]sters very much as some kitchen cabinets do, rather than having [a] conventional wardrobe system with opening doors.

Keeping all the practical elements to either side of the room [m]akes the most of the play area in the center, which is important. [Al]so, with open storage easy to hand, tidying up can be done [qu]ickly, so it is easy to persuade the children to do it.

Decorating an area for four different personalities is always [di]fficult. Originally, the eldest boy wanted a spaceship theme, [w]hile the younger ones begged for a pirate ship. Even in a fairly [bi]g room, this would have looked chaotic and untidy, so [co]mpromises were made by using blocks of color to create a [se]mi-industrial look which appealed to all the children.

The circular holes are spaceship-like, and the ladders up to the [pl]atforms could be thought to be the rigging of a pirate ship. But [th]ey all work together under the industrial theme that has been [cr]eated. Blue was eventually chosen as the main color, because it [is] a relatively calm and peaceful theme for a bedroom, and the [br]ight splashes of red and yellow are testament to its extra [fu]nction as a place for play.

4: A theme of primary colors works for books, toys, and bedlinen alike.

5: There is plenty of room for playful activities in this room.

6: Many of the toys are decorative in their own right.

7: The bed platforms are supported by wooden end pieces just short of the window. This leaves a space for a bookcase, creating useful extra storage.

bed/bath: screened off

A bedroom and bathroom divided by a screen, rather than a wall, has many of the advantages of an open-plan space without loss of privacy. There will be more light and a spacious feel in the room. Here designer and cookbook writer Alastair Hendy has used a wooden block as a room divider cum headboard, allowing light to flood in from the bathroom to the bedroom, and letting the bathroom's blue mosaics become a color feature in an otherwise neutrals-and-naturals bedroom.

A sink hangs on the other side of this giant block of wood, which also serves as a headboard. A bath, too, is virtually hidden from sight, but a reclaimed 1930s shower head and radiators (inset) can be seen from the bedroom area .

creating light

This is a very contemporary interior, but such a layout would work equally well in more traditional materials and designs, and it's an idea that can offer a real alternative to a boxlike en-suite bathroom or a completely open-plan look. One of the biggest problems about carving a bathroom out of a bedroom is the effect on the windows, and the relationship of the windows to the shape of the room both before and afterward. Here the bathroom receives almost all the natural light available to the room – apart from some borrowed light from an adjacent room via a glass brick wall – so a screen or an open-plan arrangement was essential. Even in a more conventional space the same problems may exist. For example, placing the bathroom away from the windows restricts how you place the bed, and this is when it is well worth considering using a solid, but incomplete

FLOORPLAN
(1) Closet hidden by floor to ceiling panel. (2) Similar walk-in closet/utility area.

(3) Toilet. (4) Storage chest. (5) Bed. (6) Partition. (7) Sink (8) Bath. (9) Shower.

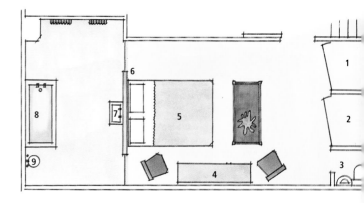

1 and 2: The ultra-modern look of the bed, situated on its platform, works very well | **with the sleek, smooth lines of the 1930s furniture.**

3: The full length floor-to-ceiling panels are doors with invisible press catches. They | **lead to a toilet, walk-in close and laundry area.**

1

2

reen. It does not have to reach the ceiling — anything just over
e height of a tall man will conceal everything satisfactorily.

There are several other good tricks in this bedroom-bathroom,
y one of which could be adopted in other rooms. One wall
pears to be three large panels — in fact, they are three floor-to-
ling flush doors, each of which presses open. One conceals the
let. Another leads into a walk-in closet with a washing machine,
yer and other equipment. The third is a closet with shelves. These
ree large "closets" mean that furniture in this room can be
inimal. Just one giant chest has pride of place.

With a bathroom area that is partially on view, there needs
be a sense of visual discipline about the way it is fitted out.
ere the theme of a 1930s public swimming pool successfully
ks the building's historic past with its current contemporary
terpretation, as 1930s design has much in common with the
ean, sweeping lines of today's modernism.

4: Drawers double as steps
that lead to the sleeping/
storage platform.

5: A wall of glass bricks
helps to bring some extra light
into the bedroom from the
stairwell area.

4

5

THE BED/BATH: SCREENED OFF CHECKLIST

■ Remember that the cost of renovation can be double or triple what you have paid in the first place.

■ Check that the item can be repaired or renovated. Refer to page 149 for lists of specialist craftsmen and organizations.

■ The weathered or aged look is part of the charm of recycled items for many people, but check the functionality carefully.

■ Spare parts are often a problem if, say, faucet sizes have changed over the decades. You may able to improvise – for example, washers are no longer made for these faucets but a piece of rubber works just as well.

■ If renovation worries you, many companies are making exactly the same designs today. You may be able to buy identical models that are new. However, many of the "Victorian-style" or "Georgian-style" items in large home centers are often cheap pastiches and best avoided if you want authenticity.

To maintain a clear view of a straight floor from the bedroom, the standard shower tray was dispensed with, so water flows from the giant shower head onto the mosaic floor. This large shower head – a genuine antique refitted for current plumbing – pumps out an enormous volume of water at any one time. This means that the drainage must be carefully assessed. Without a shower tray, it's necessary to have the tiled floor at a slope toward the drain or the bedroom may be flooded. And even with a shower tray, you can get flooding unless there is good drainage.

The bath was made of cement blocks, properly sealed to keep water out, and tiled in the same blue mosaic tiles as the rest of the room. Remember to check how slippery bathroom floor tiles are before buying.

visual links

Many fixtures, such as faucets, sinks, and radiators, are recycled from architectural salvage yards and renovated. This can prove tricky as it can be difficult to get the right washers for antique faucets, for example. In this case, the owner cut rubber washers himself, but it is usually difficult to get plumbers to agree to this. There are many professional companies that renovate salvage items such as radiators and parquet flooring (see directory), but do remember that this can add quite a lot to the cost. Slabs of marble or marble tiles, for example, can be restored by cleaning and polishing.

far right: The sloping glass roof is the only natural light available to this bedroom/bathroom, as it is situated in a basement.

1 and 2: Washers for these faucets are no longer made, but a piece of rubber, that h. been cut to fit, will work jus as well.

3: Square, simple lines and a minimum of decorative detai keep this bathroom area looking contemporary. The giant shower head is a reclaimed model from the 1930s. The bath is cement blocks, sealed to hold water, and then tiled with the same mosaic tiles that decorate th floor and the ceiling area.

4: The faucets and basin are also reclaimed architectural salvage items.

5: The toilet is hidden away neatly behind the giant door panels on the other side of t room, and is a contemporary model.

color

fragrance

roll-around storage

freestanding mirrors

Storage is the key to style and comfort. Displaying items on hangers makes them easier to find, while concealing them in boxes and drawers reduces clutter. Most bedrooms-plus benefit from a mixture of the two, but all require a place for everything to fit everything in its place.

hatboxes and bandboxes

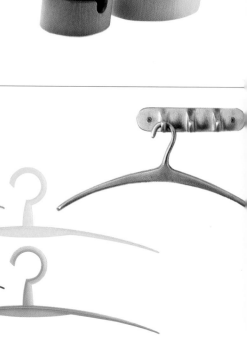

innovative shapes

exible furniture

seat cum linen basket

box storage

Use the walls: take radiators up rather than along, divide up hanging space into short and long, try out flexible hanging shelves, and hang shoes, ties, scarves, and belts. Look out for multiple hangers that take several sets of trousers, blouses, folding items, and even collapsible hanging holdalls.

ideas for hanging

esigner linoleum

dynamic towel bars

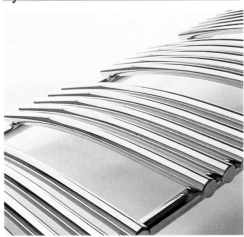

armchair to relax in

colored glycerine soaps

bedside lighting

In the bedroom comfort and functional excellence must be balanced because a good night's sleep is as important as a healthy diet. A well designed bed is one that offers perfect rest as well as useful extras. Check out the soft elements: chairs, blankets, bedlinen – these are the definers of luxury.

beautiful bedlinen

cozy blankets

sheer comfort

innovative furniture

hests of drawers

drawers for bulky items

lling storage unit

Chests of drawers can be large or small, portable or stationary, antique or contemporary, but varying sizes and shapes of drawers are useful. Bathroom storage is essential to reduce clutter – either borrowed from other parts of the house or customized for the bathroom.

bathroom storage

compartment storage

VERTICAL

LIVING

You can often carve valuable extra living space out of a house if you think vertically. Halls and stairways, basements and mezzanine areas could all be used for storage, shower rooms, sitting or relaxing areas, or sites for home offices. Bookcases, for example, built just the width of a book, can be positioned along the narrowest of corridors or down a slender space such as around a door or under a window. And don't forget the roof – either open it up for double height rooms or fit cupboards and hatches for long-term storage.

Although the spaces are small, it is worth taking the extra time, trouble and, if necessary, spending extra money to ensure that they are exactly right. When every inch counts, you can't afford mistakes: check measurements, act out movements within the space (for example, to check whether a tall person can stand or reach easily) and make sure you understand exactly what the result will be.

the understairs/ office

This compact home office makes maximum use of the space under the stairs that is often forgotten or treated as a dumping ground. Instead of a stair rail, there are shelves reaching from floor to ceiling (inset), allowing light in from the floor above. A comprehensive storage system is tucked into the stair treads at several levels, from low cupboards at the base to eye-level shelving. A vibrant color scheme based on ocher and blue adds warmth to the area.

Using open shelving against the stairs instead of a banister makes the most of the vertical space. Here, these shelves are open to either the stairs or the hallway, but they could also be backed with sheets of toughened or frosted glass, or colored Perspex without cutting out light.

Defining the space

Every part of this area under the stairs has been used to its maximum capacity in a design by architect Melissa Merryweather. It is an exceptionally tight corner to work in, which meant that careful – and absolutely accurate – plans were critical, with every aspect worked out finely to the last measurement before any structural work took place. Such a task is easier if the stairs are being built or rebuilt at the time, as the steps and the rise can be made to work with the design, but this is not essential.

First, establish what you need in terms of head height and reach. It is completely impossible to work in an area if you hit your head on a stair tread every time you lean forward. It is also important to feel sure that you'll be happy with the way the stairs slope overhead, and that you won't find it claustrophobic.

Then list everything you plan to do in the office, and how long you plan to spend there at any one time. This one is both a home office and a "command control center" for the house, containing all the domestic bills and papers as well as work. It is used for an estimated 4–8 hours a week, although no one spends more than an hour or so at a time at the desk. This establishes where compromises can be made. In such a confined space, for example,

it is not possible to have a full desk surface and an ergonomically correct office chair with a back, but, because it will only be used for short periods, a space-saving stool can be substituted instead to leave a relatively generous desk area.

There could be no compromises on storage, however, and by measuring the wall and stair space accurately it was possible to pack a surprising number of boxes and baskets into a very small area. There needed to be a gap for feet, knees, and legs under the main part of the desk, but there was room for storage at the side. Big boxes are set on the floor with a shelf for document boxes above. At eye level above the desk there is a shelf for files, while below, where the stair treads recede, are two open shelves and a deep cupboard for general items such as stationery and record books. There is room for a few more files, plus CD-ROM and disk boxes on the desktop and the shelves by the staircase.

1: Neatly labeled box files are ideal storage in a small space. Choose different colored ones for easy identification.

2: This shelving is structurally supporting the room above, and would normally be a solid wall, making the hall darker.

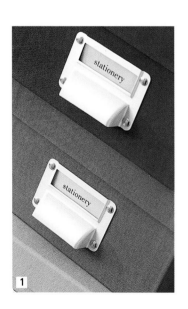

Stool. (2) Desk area.
Files on the shelves and in
e cupboard built into the
air treads. (4) Telephone
ea. (5) Area for the
mputer. (6) Box files on top
 desk area, with two extra
elves of storage situated
neath. (7) Open shelving
at replaced stair banisters.
Stairs to room up above.

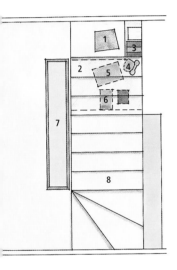

Light is a major issue in small, awkward spaces such as this. Some natural light is essential, and if even the tiniest window can be carved out of the wall, then this will make a great deal of difference. Otherwise use "borrowed" light, such as here where the daylight streams in from the sky lights above the staircase. Most hallways and stairways have some access to sunlight. Good electric lighting is essential too – low-voltage halogen spotlights equate most closely to natural daylight, and, as there may not be room for a desk lamp, check that the spotlights can angle light where you will need it without creating glare on the computer screen. Fire precautions are important in hallways and stairways, so the spotlights shown here are in fireproof housing, and wherever possible fireproof materials have been used.

Understairs spaces are also very much on view to everyone passing through the house, so here there has been a deliberate policy to use warm, strong colors in a palette of ocher, gray and blue. It is well worth investing in some stylish storage boxes and files, or at least coordinating them.

3: The deep cupboard is fitted into the stair treads. Note the low-voltage halogen lightbulb set in to the tread above.

4, 5 and 6: Shelves at different heights can maximize storage: vases and bottles for the living area can be housed above.

■ There is no room for mistakes. Take yourself through a day at the desk, and make sure you would be comfortable. Measure out all your actions. For example, sitting at the desk, leaning forward, and standing up. Check your head room and elbow room against the stair tread and the walls.

■ Measure the space you need for desk, storage, and chair. Can you get them all in? Where can you compromise? If you intend to work long hours, you will need an adjustable office chair with good back support. It should be on casters and be able to swivel.

■ Have electrical outlets put in for a computer, fax, printer, and answering machine. Do not rely on an extension cord from an entry hall outlet, as trailing wires are dangerous.

■ Fit good lighting. All electrical equipment should be fireproofed.

■ Measure the space for shelves and storage accurately. Allow for large and small boxes, using the full height and width of available wall space as a grid.

the mezzanine/ living space

The principal difficulty with converting basements is that there is often little access to natural light. Many units in the basement were originally designed for storage rather than living, and this apartment – converted from an old printing factory – is a prime example. By cutting out a "well" area, light was borrowed from the floor-to-ceiling windows on the ground floor, opening up the space and illuminating beautifully the stylish open-plan kitchen beneath.

A narrow mezzanine walkway leading to an open staircase provides access to the kitchen level. For those working in the kitchen (inset) this means a double-height space, while there is a warren of cabinets that provide some useful storage in the darker areas at the side of the room.

creative planning

The owner, cookbook writer and designer Alastair Hendy, decided to sacrifice a chunk of the ground floor in order to open up the whole of the basement. He cut a hole in the floor, with access via a mezzanine walkway and stairs. This meant light could stream in from the floor-to-ceiling windows on the ground floor, and, by changing the panes of the narrow slit to match these windows, he was able to make it look part of one long light source. This created a security problem as windows at ground or basement level are vulnerable to being broken, so he installed a metal grille, similar to those used in shops and businesses. This slides down at the touch of a button to provide privacy or security.

The result of lengthening the window and removing part of the floor is a kitchen with a double-height ceiling in its working and eating area. This well is large and bright, and throws light onto storage and cooking areas at the sides, which have their original ceilings. Removing part of a floor could also make a basement with a low ceiling a viable living space. A cut-out well is worth considering in many instances – it may sacrifice more of the floor above, but it can create a really good, light working area.

The light well also offered the option of creating a second roo — a bedroom-bathroom (see pages 94–99) with light "borrowe from this well, using a wall of glass bricks between the kitch and the bedroom. In these rooms he also used another device increasing the light. At one side there was an area where t basement extended farther to the side of the building than t walls of the ground floor, and by roofing this extra space w translucent (not transparent) glass, light pours in from overhe Overhead light is always the most effective – a small overhe hatch window will give as much light as a larger side windo Sometimes it's possible to extend a basement area out into t garden, and with a glass roof you'll get a light, open room.

By sinking the kitchen down into the open well, this masks it from the main living room, and makes it less than open-plan, b accessible. This means that the relaxing/living zone upstairs is fr from the sight of cooking clutter, although from the mezzani walkway both rooms can be seen. This demands strong visual lin such as using professional catering materials in both areas, alo with bold, big pieces of furniture and minimal color.

1: A contemporary, industrial theme in tune with the building has been chosen to link the downstairs kitchen and upstairs living area.

2: The stairway down to the kitchen is simple and open.

FLOORPLAN
(1) Living area with sofas and fireplace. (2) Mezzanine platform. (3) Stairs down to kitchen. (4) Food preparation and sink. (5) Food preparation zone. (6) Range. (7) Leading to storage under stairs.

■ Even a small amount of natural light will make a big difference to the success of a room. Try to create a "well" somewhere, either by removing floor space from above, or by digging out toward the garden.

■ Light from above is more effective than side windows, so a small well or lantern light overhead will be as effective as a window four times the size.

■ Try to "borrow" light when you divide the room up. Consider using glass bricks or sandblasted glass partitions instead of solid walls.

■ Even the stairs will have some effect on light: metal rails will allow more to come through than a solid banister.

■ Don't forget security – basement areas can be accessible and therefore vulnerable to burglars.

■ Consider ventilation and damp-proofing. Going ahead without covering the formalities will cause problems when you try to sell.

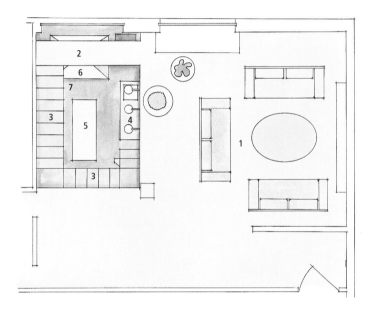

3, 4 and 5: The kitchen is effectively open-plan to the living room, but as it is on a level below the kitchen, clutter is concealed from the living area. These photographs show how the space was cut from the ground floor and how the mezzanine walkway and stairs curve around and down.

the landing/office

A great deal can be made of a small area in a hallway or on a landing. These slivers of space – often left over from a more leisurely age when builders and home-owners could afford to be extravagant – can be just the right size to take a desk, chest, or chair. The hallway usually offers a light well that affects the atmosphere of the whole house, so if you can make the space work without cutting out sunlight then you will create something usable that will leave your home feeling light and spacious.

A light and airy corner of a hallway offers the opportunity for a useful home work zone that is used occasionally, rather than a full-scale office.

By organizing the desk and storage properly (inset), it is surprising how much you can fit in and also do in such a restricted space.

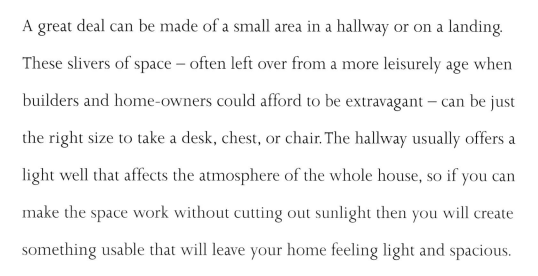

The desk is narrow enough to prevent the chair from constantly being in the way of people going up and down the stairs.

a basic office

This desk zone had been converted into a tiny bathroom by previous tenant, and, by opening it up, the owners restored light of a huge window to the landing. This kind of set up is the person who only works at home intermittently – anyo trying to run a business from such a restricted area would so feel frustrated. Also, for prolonged typing, the computer scre and keyboard should not be at the same height. But for the pers who just needs a parking place for bills and correspondence, who has children who may want to use it for homework, it take the pressure off other rooms in the house.

a quick, easy desk

It is unlikely that you will find exactly the right piece of furnit to fit in between the walls, but this doesn't have to me commissioning anything complicated. For example, something simple as a piece of wood or laminated ply, cut to measure, th rested on file cabinets will be both practical and inexpensi

FLOORPLAN
(1) Window. (2) Desk. (3) Computer.
(4) File cabinet. (5) Chair. (6) Stairs.

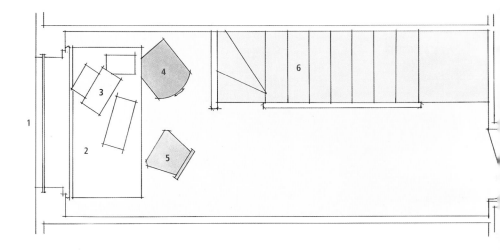

ockists of kitchen countertops are a good place to start, as you ll need a fairly strong surface, and certainly one that won't arp or bend. Wood of the required thickness, such as beech, can surprisingly inexpensive, or consider laminates – these are w available in a wide range of colors and finishes. If you're ing to be using a personal computer at the desk, there are two ings to bear in mind before ordering the surface. First, make re that the measurements you specify include the depth of the mputer plus the keyboard. Second, remember that there is ten quite a substantial amount of wiring to be taken into count. This should ideally run down the back of the desk, rather an trailing over your working surface, so you may want to have les cut at the back, or simply leave a gap between the back of e work surface and the wall.

As people will be walking past this area every day, it's essential make it look as good as possible. Plan all your storage carefully, d make sure that there is a box, basket, or file for everything at you will need. Don't forget to include a wastepaper basket – s a surprisingly simple thing but is very useful and can be only o easy to overlook.

Pretty boxes for mundane ems such as stamps or large perclips help keep the area oking good.

Bright light streams in to the desk. This can cause distracting glare on the mputer, so it is best to fit roller shade or miniblinds ther than curtains. nstantly pulling curtains ross risks knocking things f the desk.

3: Keeping an informal color scheme, such as all-brights, pastels, or whites, for file cabinets and furniture will help pull the work zone together. Incorporating a bright file cabinet in an otherwise neutral scheme will only draw the eye unnecessarily and emphasize the clutter.

THE LANDING/OFFICE CHECKLIST

■ Make sure that chairs, corners of desks, tables, or file cabinets don't block the normal movement of people, especially when you're using the desk area. It is annoying, and potentially dangerous, to have a chair obstructing a hallway.

■ Even if the space is restricted, it should be comfortable to work at. Aspects to consider include desk height, chair height, amount of work surface available, and access to storage.

■ Make sure that all cords and plugs are out of sight and behind the desk. Trailing cords are dangerous, because people can trip over them, especially in parts of the house that they may be rushing through.

■ Keep decorative elements simple – this is not the place for elaborate curtains or fussy displays of china, as things will get knocked over.

■ If you can't find a suitable desk, have a length of wood or laminate work surface cut to fit and balance them on file cabinets.

the landing/ sitting room

This sunny spot on the top floor of a small cottage is an open space that seems, at first sight, to be a serene and relaxing corner. In fact, it's a very hard-working area, providing extensive storage space for the nearby bedrooms and a cozy reading nook for those who want to get away from the pace of life in the rest of the house. A light well also successfully opens up what would otherwise have been a very small, boxlike cottage.

Two bedrooms open directly into what was the main bedroom of the cottage. Now it is a peaceful den (inset) lined almost invisibly with essential storage. Having closets and chests of drawers on the landing also helps to keep the bedrooms free and uncluttered.

an open space

This home was made from two small workers' cottages which have been knocked together. One of the original cottages had one main bedroom, which opened up directly from the stairs without any kind of wall or door as separation, and two tiny bedrooms leading off it. Its mirror image is on the other side, and there is a door cut into the wall to connect the two. Many owners might have walled this top area off to make a third bedroom, but the effect would have been to make the top floor feel dark and boxlike. It seems an indulgence to leave it open-plan, but with extensive closets built discreetly into the walls and several chests of drawers, it offers plenty of storage space when left open-plan as well as making the atmosphere much lighter and brighter. Having the chests of drawers and closets just outside the two little bedrooms they serve also means that the bedrooms can be kept clean and simple, with just a bed and side table as furnishings.

attention to detail

Both the closets and the door to the other side of the cottage are flush with the walls and have been kept as plain as possible, with spring-catches instead of handles, so that they look like walls rather than closets. Every bit of space has been used, with smaller closets built in under the eaves of the sloping roof, and it features varyingly graduated shelving to insure maximum capacity.

Cottage windows are often difficult to curtain, with their deepset, irregularly shaped areas. Here a simple scalloped cornice, edged with braid, follows the line of the window recess without being fussy. The primrose check design echoes the innocent rural charm of the cottage. A gentle creamy-white paint is in keeping with the age of the building, as bright, brilliant whites were not invented until the 1920s. It also helps to maximize sunlight. The furnishings have been kept deliberately fresh and unpretentious too — it would not be appropriate to have expensive, lavish fabrics and furnishings in a cottage that was built several hundred years ago for very humble inhabitants. Checks and stripes against the

rich patina of beautiful old wood create a look that is bo[th] timeless and contemporary. Another important point is that the[re] aren't too many decorative elements. Apart from the white pai[nt] and the wood on the chair arms and on the chests, there is on[ly] the bright, cheerful yellow and a collection of blue jars and po[ts]. Too many colors or patterns fighting for space and air would ha[ve] made the area less peaceful and harmonious.

Great attention to detail has been paid in this tiny area. Th[e] stair uprights, for example, have been cut to a design created b[y] the owner, and the radiator is hidden by painted wooden sla[ts] with a small shelf above. The original beam in the ceiling h[as] been left exposed to emphasize the uneven lines of the cottage.

FLOORPLAN
(1) Closets. (2) Window.
(3) and (4) Pine chests.
(5) Chairs. (6) Table.
(7) Stairs. (8) Entrance.

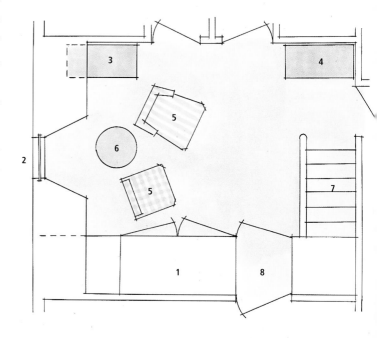

1 and 2: The cupboards are featureless and flush with the walls so they are completely unobtrusive.

Shelving is taken right under the eaves to make the most of the storage space in this old cottage.

4: A simple, cheerful window treatment and a slatted radiator cover are contemporary, but they also fit in well with the overall cottage style.

5: A collection of blue and white Chinese jars is virtually the only decorative element in this understated color scheme.

THE LANDING/SITTING ROOM CHECKLIST

■ If you want to keep storage discreet in living areas, keep decorative detail on cabinets and drawers to a bare minimum. Spring-catch doors, instead of handles, leave surfaces flush.

■ In a restricted space, fittings are highly noticeable. Banisters, stair rails, and radiator covers, for example, do not need to match, but it will make the space seem calmer if they work together decoratively.

■ Equally, fabrics, curtain treatments, and flooring will look less cluttered in a limited space if they follow a common theme.

■ Think about whether you want the furnishings to link with your home's historical past or provide a contrast with it.

■ Pale or cheerful colors and white paint, with light floors, will make the space seem lighter and airier. Dark carpets or floorboards will just darken a small space.

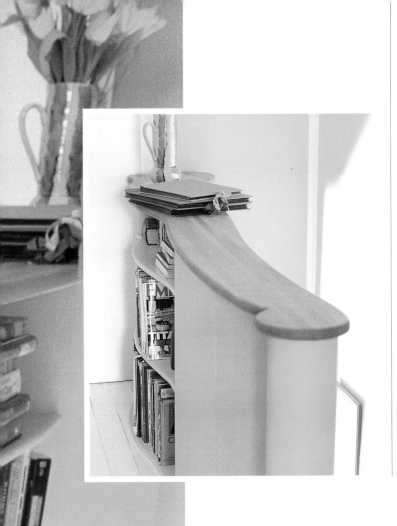

the staircase/ library

The stairs in this two-story apartment have been used for storage all the way. At the bottom, where they open out into the living room, drawers and cupboards have been installed to house an entire sound system, TV, and associated equipment, while bookcases replace banisters as the stairs begin to rise. There is the optimum use of space, with every drawer, shelf, and cabinet carefully planned and measured to make sure that no usable area is wasted.

This bookcase replaces the previous banister of the staircase entirely. It has been built with three different depths of shelves to take varying sizes of books. At its narrowest, the bookcase can store just paperbacks, but at the back it can take much larger volumes.

■ You can transform your house by organizing the storage of books, tapes, CDs, magazines, videos, and tapes properly.

■ To avoid losing any floor space in your home, look at where shelves can be built in. These take up less room than freestanding bookcases or cupboards and can be fitted into surprisingly small corners or narrow hallways.

■ Measure shelf and cabinet heights accurately, taking into account the size of large books (for example, illustrated coffee-table books), smaller books, and paperbacks.

■ Avoid having deep cabinets where you have to search for things. If a space is deep (for example, under a flight of stairs) build drawers instead as they can be pulled out for easy access. Even a tiny drawer could hold a couple of dozen tapes or a store of back-up computer disks.

utilizing space

The key to the success of this design was to measure everything accurately. There are drawers that are exactly the right size for videos or music tapes, making it much easier to find them, than when you have to hunt around in the back of a cabinet, particularly considering the width of a stairway. The TV and music system have customized slots with holes drilled for the wiring, and the bookshelves have been measured to take three sizes of books — small paperbacks, large paperbacks, and illustrated, coffee-table tomes. There is also some further shelf space for accessories. To tie in with the rest of the room, it was painted in a shade of pale orange.

Using the space under the stairs for storage works best if it is carefully calculated. There is a piece of Japanese furniture called a *kaidan-dansu*, which is a chest of drawers built in a stepped fashion

1: Curves in the design of the bookcase give it a flowing, streamlined look and make it appear less formal.

2: Cleverly designed, built-in storage under the stairs houses all the music and TV equipment.

3: Small drawers are very handy to have. They are easy to keep tidy, and they hold a surprisingly large amount of CDs and tapes.

FLOORPLAN
(1) Bookcase and storage under stairs. (2) Stairs.
(3) Bookcase on landing.

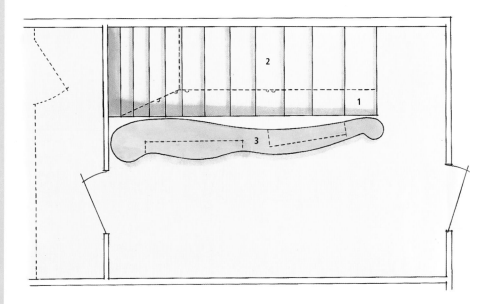

se stairs. It's a format that can offer helpful tips in Western design – try building drawers into the side of stairs so that they ll out into the room. As the stairs rise, there is room for nging things or tall objects, and you gain a great deal of extra rage by building varying sizes of cabinets to fit different-sized jects. This is better than making one big cabinet or standard zes of shelves and trying to store everything away haphazardly. any people use this kind of understairs space for storing ashing machines or microwaves, in which case you can build propriate storage in the surrounding space to take all the cessary washing detergent, ingredients, or china.

xtra storage

he same stairs have been used to increase the number of ookshelves, and these have been built in place of the banisters. t the bottom of the banister the shelves are just the width of a aperback book, plus a little extra, and there is access to them from the stair side. At the top, larger books can be accommodated and these can be reached from the landing.

The bookcase was made by cutting a curved piece of wood, with a central slot, and attaching it to the newel posts. A second piece of wood slotted into this, and shelves were screwed in between. A piece of kitchen countertop in beech made a broad top to the whole bookcase, and provides a useful halfway house for laundry and other household items. This bookcase was then painted yellow to link it in with the bathroom upstairs and to contrast with a blue bedroom that leads off the upper landing.

Even the narrowest of halls and corridors can often be made to work harder by using such techniques, and books, in particular, take up very little space when stored vertically. One successful trick is to run a bookcase around a doorway – above it and on either side of it – so the door appears deepset. If the depth of the shelves is a bit more than that of a paperback book, the impact on floor space is negligible, yet many books can be accommodated.

into the roof: kitchen/ living room

An attic space between the roof and the ceilings below can be more than just a place to store clutter. Removing the ceilings on the top floor, then carving a slice of vertical space out of part of the room can be an exciting and practical way to create a stunning interior. Here a living room with a mezzanine kitchen makes a lively, light, and easy-to-live-with double-use room.

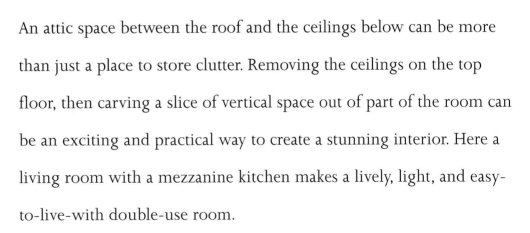

A dining table overlooks the living area. It can be seen from below (inset) and is a sociable eating and working space, while also being separated enough to keep the clutter of cooking and eating out of sight. Extra light is provided by skylights, giving the room a sunny feel.

Innovative solutions

Houses with sloping roofs are to be found all over the world. The slice of space between the ceiling of the top floor and the roof is normally the storage area. Hundreds of unwanted items and bulky suitcases are shoved up there year after year, and usually forgotten. If there is enough space, an extra living floor may be possible, but very often there isn't quite enough head height to do this, and restrictive covenants may mean that the outside roof level cannot be taken up. However, there are several ways of using the attic for something more exciting than a giant junk room.

First, consider what you can do if you remove the ceiling, exposing the roof to the room below. At the very least this will transform a room with a low ceiling into a magnificent vaulted room. You may not be using that extra height for anything, but it will make the whole room feel more spacious.

Second, depending on how the stairs rise and what the layout of the top floor is, you may be able to use some of the full-height space in the attic. This may not be as large as a whole room, but it could make a difference to how the top floor works. A shower and a toilet carved out of ceiling space over a stairwell, for example, and reached by a short half-flight of stairs from the top floor, could create an extra bathroom without breaking up a bedroom.

If there is a little more space to work with, a mezzanine level can increase a house's floor area and add an extra "room". Here a mezzanine floor has been created over one side of the living room, leaving a double-height ceiling on the other side. This mezzanine is a kitchen, but it could also be a bedroom or a dining or study platform. Had these two living spaces been walled off, they would have been strange, boxlike rooms. There is also the problem that most mezzanine areas, even if they are high enough for a tall man, do not have enough head height to constitute a proper room. As an all-in-one-space the area is sociable, spacious, and light, and keeps the cooking and living areas separate but connected.

While adding an extra room or floor to a house is often problematic or even impossible, simply carving out a mezzanine

in the roof area is unlikely to meet resistance. This is because the is no change to the exterior of the house, although, in a few are you may need permission to add skylights or roof windows, ev if they're flush with the line of the roof. Otherwise the structu aspect is relatively straightforward. Do remember that hot rises. In winter this makes heating the rooms easier, as heat w rise from the rest of the house, but you should talk to yo builder about having an extra layer of insulation to prevent it fr escaping altogether. In the summer, heat may be a problem, make sure that there are several windows that will open provide ventilation. When windows are in the roof, they a relatively secure, so if you like to leave them open often, choose design that doesn't allow a rainstorm to drench your home!

This mezzanine formula works well with most designs. In th house white paint, white seating, and simple painted wood crea a fresh, airy feel and maximize the sunlight. Although it is in busy city street, you could easily be at the beach or in the countr

t: The kitchen area is
inted in soft colors to give it
living-room feel. The original
tic was not really high
ough to stand up in, but by
moving the ceiling and
pping the ceiling height of
e room below on one side of
at room, an extra half-floor
fitted in. It doesn't feel
ustrophobic because of the
uble-height ceiling on the
her side of the room.

ht: White armchairs and
ished floorboards maintain
e simple, uncluttered
mosphere of the kitchen area.

OOR PLAN
Living area. (2) Raised
ezzanine for cooking/dining.
Run of kitchen cabinets.
Dining table. (5) Banister
erlooking living area.

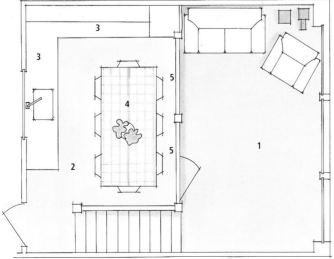

■ Although simply removing ceilings is not difficult and shouldn't cause any structural problems, it is often a good idea to use an architect to plan the space properly.

■ Heating and ventilation are critical here. Allow enough windows for a good flow-through of air, and an extra layer of insulation to prevent heat loss.

■ Windows flush to the roof, such as Velux, let in more light than dormer windows. You may not be able to add dormer windows because of restictive covenants.

■ Another excellent way of flooding the room with light is to replace a section of the roof with insulated solarium glass.

■ Don't neglect safety with mezzanine banister rails. They should be secure enough for a baby or toddler not to fall through.

■ If you put a shower in this space you will need extra plumbing. With a new toilet, take care with placing the soil pipe, as there are often restrictions on their location.

color

stackable furniture

Small spaces can often benefit from large furniture. Choose chests for the optimum size of drawer – storage is often more effective when divided up into small manageable chunks. Sculptural, simple shapes in furniture prevent halls and mezzanines from looking cluttered.

different-size drawers

pedestal tables

ays of hiding technology

compact club-style chairs

special sizes of radiators

ace-saving stool

Time spent choosing exactly the right shape and size of furniture to make the most of an awkward corner will pay off in all areas, from chests and tables to chairs and radiators. The choice today is extensive – there are radiators for the narrowest strip of wall, and comfortable chairs for the most compact space.

eye-catching flooring

hard-wearing carpet

hanging shelving

Stairs and hallways feel more spacious when incorporated decoratively into the body of the house, while continuous color and floor treatments create a feeling of flowing, open space. Even a few square feet of wall can house some extra shelves, split into compartments to keep items separate.

chevron stripes

inspired design

ldaway furniture

decorative shelving

xtensive shelving

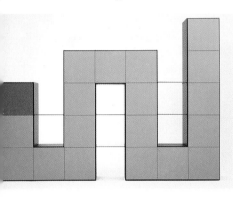

Foldaway furniture, either built-in or freestanding, can turn a small corner into a room, and suspending items from walls frees up floor space. Hallways and mezzanines are on display from most rooms in the house – simple shapes work well with decorative schemes elsewhere in the house.

mple shapes

CONSERVATORY

PLUS

Conservatories can either be all-year rooms – provided that they have double-glazing with good heating and ventilation – or summer-only rooms with less stringent requirements. They can be living or dining rooms, kitchens or corridors linking one part of a building to another, or you can replace part of a roof with conservatory glass to make a breathtaking room in the sky. Conservatories add extra floor space at ground level if part of the house wall is removed and supported with steel joists. They can fill the dead space between a house and its garden wall, or add an extra story higher up.

Check several manufacturers or builders before committing yourself (using the tips on pages 134-137) and try to ensure that companies are both financially sound and experienced. To use the room properly, it is essential to plan the shape and the siting of the doors and windows carefully, so don't feel you have to accept a standard design.

country style: kitchen/dining/ conservatory

Adding a conservatory is often the best way of opening up dark or difficult rooms, or creating extra space for your household. This is a huge garden room cum kitchen, dining room and living area. It allows the family to enjoy their country garden all year round, and has been planned as a versatile space with a cooking zone and a separate "wet" area just off it. All appliances, such as fridge, freezer, and TV, are hidden inside custom-made cabinets.

Natural materials – bare brick, granite countertops, beech flooring – link the room with the garden in a contemporary way. The central island (inset) is a food preparation area, with its own sink. The cooking range is behind the pillars and the doorway leads to a small dishwashing and storage area.

A flexible space

This is a large room, but it still needs careful planning. The temptation in bigger kitchens is to spread everything out, and this usually results in a room that is exhausting to work in and lacks flexibility. Here all the cooking is done in approximately one-quarter of the space, and there is literally one step from the food preparation area to the cooking range, and three steps to the dishwashing and china storage area. This not only makes life easier for the cook, but also leaves the maximum amount of space free in the rest of the room for playing, dining, or entertaining.

The central island is not, in fact, central, but is set to one side. It is the food preparation zone, with a granite countertop, giant chopping board, garbage disposal unit, a sink for rinsing, washing, and adding water, and a breakfast bar with stools. Just beside it is a handsome, custom-made pantry cupboard, which houses the fridge, microwave, and television. Keeping all these elements hidden gives it much more of a living room feel.

The main sink, along with the dishwasher and all the storage for glass, china, and flatware is in a small alcove off the main room – what would previously have been called a butler's pantry. This convenient arrangement hides dirty dishes or pans awaiting washing from sight, and also means that the person doing the dishes and the cook need not get in each other's way. Most importantly, it means that unloading the dishwasher or putting things away after drying them on the draining board requires no more than opening a cabinet and stretching out an arm.

an all-year room

Building a conservatory that will be an all-year room requires planning and investment. Too many conservatories are merely greenhouses tacked onto the sides of buildings, with inadequate heating and ventilation. These issues are critical, or you will waste your money. While it is more expensive to build a conservatory properly, it is good value for money if it adds another room to your house or makes your current space more usable. Conversely

Having the sink, dishwasher, glass storage, and china cabinets all together in the "wet area" off the main conservatory cuts down on walking around an otherwise large room.

FLOORPLAN

(1) Doors from living room. (2) Dining table. (3) Central island. (4) Extra sink, garbage disposal unit, and chopping board. (5) Range and cooktop. (6) Wet area off main conservatory. (7) Main sink. (8) Dishwasher. (9)·Cabinets for glass and china. (10) Armoire for fridge, television, and dry food storage. (11) Doors to garden.

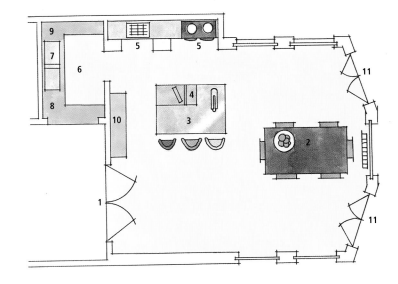

and 2: Custom-made ᴠooden cabinets in a ᴄontemporary style neatly ᴏuse all the kitchen ᴘaraphernalia and appliances, ᴤuch as the microwave.

3, 4 and 5: To soften the sleek look of the modern kitchen equipment, it has been fitted next to or built into natural time-honored materials such as granite, brick, and wood.

COUNTRY STYLE: KITCHEN/DINING/ CONSERVATORY CHECKLIST

■ Choose a conservatory with a good-qualtiy construction. Don't just buy a standard package without checking that it offers all that's needed: double glazing and toughened glass are essential for heating/security reasons. Polycarbonate roofs are cheaper, but brittle, noisier and opaque. Double-glazed roofs are more expensive, but can be repaired and look better.

■ Ventilation is the key: you need to be able to open several windows in the roof plus one-third of the side windows. Side-opening windows are better than top-hanging ones.

■ Consider the effect of the shape on usable space. Rectangles and squares offer more space and flexibility. Bay-shaped conservatories limit furniture placement.

■ Make a scale drawing of the conservatory and furniture, and work out a room plan before finalizing the design.

■ Central doors cut down usable space. Try using side doors instead.

you may waste what is still a large sum of money if you buy a cheap conservatory, and only use it for a few weeks a year.

There are, essentially two kinds of conservatories. One is a self-contained room on the back or side of the house, with the original doorway to the garden maintained as a door between house and conservatory. The second is when part of the back or side wall of a room is removed and the conservatory is added to make an existing room, such as a kitchen, larger and lighter. Either can work well, but it is worth deciding which would suit you better. This conservatory/kitchen/dining room is the latter type, creating a large, free-flowing space. This is also a technique that works well on a far smaller scale: a small, dark kitchen can be completely transformed by removing one wall and replacing it with even a small 10-foot (3-meter) deep conservatory.

Look at several different plans before you agree on a shape. It may sound premature to say that you should know where every piece of furniture will go before the first brick is laid, but it is the only way to insure that you get what you want. Make a simple plan of the conservatory at a scale of 1 foot to 1 inch (300mm to 25mm) for example – and then cut out scaled-down pieces of paper to show furniture (such as your dining table, side tables, armchairs, or sofa). Use these to try out a few different room layouts, and see how flexible the room will be. A point to note is that a bay shape gives you less wall space than a rectangular or square conservatory, so that if you choose a bay shape your only option may be a small table in the center. It's also worth considering the position of the door. If it is straight ahead, then people going out to the garden will cut across living space. It may be better to have a side door. Discuss these issues with your conservatory designer, bearing in mind that you're the one who's going to live in the house, and if they just want to sell you their standard package, you may get better value elsewhere.

Next, consider the structure. Double glazing (using toughened glass) is essential if you want to use the room all year round, and, if you have opened up a wall to the house, it will also make the conservatory as secure as any other room in the house. If the conservatory is north-facing, the glass should also be "low-e" or

above: There's no need to use conservatory furniture – your home will be more flexible if tables and chairs can also be used elsewhere in the house.

below: In a room designed in sleek, contemporary style, a few more exuberant touches, such as fitting a candelabra, can look especially good.

ow emissivity", which reflects heat back into the room, but this n't necessary if it is south facing. Your conservatory dealer ould fit you with good window locks and a five-leverlock (as r front doors) for the doors to the garden.

The roof can be made of either polycarbonate or double- glazed ass. Polycarbonate is much cheaper, but it is opaque, very noisy the rain, and eventually goes brittle (after about 10 years), hen it can't be repaired. Double glazing looks better, is less noisy d, provided the wood has been properly treated, will last longer. lso, if panes of glass do crack, they can be repaired, so the ructure will last a lifetime or more. Opt for safety glass that has a m which will hold the glass in place if it breaks (this is rare, but tree may lose branches in a major storm). The roof should have a ope of at 15 degrees, or you will get weather damage. If that is ot possible (because of windows, for example) have a flat tumen roof with a roof lantern in the center.

Conservatories can be made of softwoods or non-endangered ardwoods. Agbar, for example, is a hardwood that is approved by riends of the Earth. Ideally, use hardwoods because they don't ontract and expand as much as softwoods, and the extremes of eat and cold in a conservatory can be greater than normal. oftwoods can be treated to make them more suitable.

Ventilation is absolutely critical to a comfortable conservatory. ou should be able to open several roof hatches (depending on e size of the roof) and at least one-third of the side windows ould be openable. Side-opening windows give better ventilation an top-hanging ones.

Once you have the double glazing and ventilation sorted out, en heating is straightforward. Radiators can be added onto your ntral heating system, or underfloor heating can be installed. The tter is comfortable, especially with tiles, stone, or wood ooring, but it may demand more piping than your heating stem can maintain.

When it comes to furnishings, you don't need to have "garden rniture". As this example shows, any furniture made of natural aterials looks good. And if you're short of space, then you'll ant furniture that can also be used elsewhere in the house.

right: This conservatory/ kitchen/dining room links house and garden, contemporary and traditional, with the use of old brick and traditional window bars. Ivy provides some interesting, year-round greenery.

below: Wood, stone, terra-cotta or ceramic tiles are good choices for conservatories, but should be protected with a good sealant.

city style: patio/dining/ conservatory

A conservatory-dining room on the roof of a back addition transforms this two-story city apartment built over a store by giving it outside space and more room for entertaining. An ingenious use of mirrors makes the narrow area, surrounded on three sides by walls, look larger than it is, and it is linked to the living zone (inset) by a decorative theme strictly limited to metal, glass, wood, and white.

Using the same materials (metal, glass, and wood) to link the conservatory with the living room means that furniture can be switched easily between either area. Here the table looks equally good laid for a summer lunch in the conservatory or decorated with flowers in the main room.

outside

This two-story apartment situated above a store is narrow and deep, and, with buildings on either side, it was originally quite dark. As there was no access to a garden, the owner, floral designer Stephen Woodhams, wanted to create an outside space for summer dining, with a small enclosed "courtyard" on the remainder of the roof. Working with architect Peter Romaniuk, they designed a small conservatory to sit on top of the back addition of the store below, opening up the kitchen area so that the space and air flows through all year round.

Siting a conservatory on a roof places great demands on the structure, and in this case the load was too heavy for the building

to bear. The solution, devised by Romaniuk, was to attach t sheets of toughened glass to 12 steel beams. These beams a supported by the walls on either side, so that the weight of t conservatory is taken by both side walls as well as the ro spreading the load.

The conservatory was drawn into the main room very simp by removing the window between it and the kitchen, and also removing what had been a door onto the roof. This not on makes it easy to chat between the kitchen and the conservato but also improves the flow of air around the apartment on h days. This is a factor to consider if you're adding a greenhouse conservatory to the back of a building. Conservatories are le secure than brick houses, but there are metal security grilles t can be extended across the window and door, and can be lock

The flooring (1, 2 and 3) combines a steel mesh, which allows lights to be set in underfoot, with metal "factory floor" sheets. The sophisticated lighting system, plus a control for the doors, is operated by a panel of dimmer switches (4), including one that turns the glass doors from clear to opaque (far left). In this instance it operates merely as an experimental visual effect – the glass of the conservatory is clear on either side of it – but where privacy is an issue, it could be used in glass doors to abolish the need for curtains, shades, or blinds.

left: When adding a conservatory to a small space it is essential to have furniture that sits equally happily inside or out, as extra sets of tables and chairs will make the house feel more cramped. These dining chairs and table are also used inside, but when they are in the conservatory the main room feels much more open and spacious.

CITY STYLE: PATIO/DINING/ CONSERVATORY CHECKLIST

■ A contemporary style can use toughened or laminated sheet glass bolted onto steel joists rather than a frame. This is best used in small space with an attractive view as there is no timber or brick to interrupt the eyeline. Larger conservatories need frames, as huge sheets of glass are too heavy.

■ Glass should be either toughened (which shatters on breaking) or laminated (which crazes or cracks but stays in place). Some people use a combination.

■ These conservatories are rarely double-glazed – it's too expensive and solid-looking.

■ Consult an architect on the positioning (eg whether it gets or needs direct sunlight). Check ventilation. Large doors here blow air through the door and window space at the back.

hen the house is empty. When not in use, these slide right back nd are virtually invisible.

The other clever trick was to maximize light and space by sing giant mirrors on the two side walls of the conservatory. eel sheets hang at an angle to the mirrored walls, leaving a arrow triangular strip for Stephen Woodhams's stunning floral esigns, which are changed regularly each season. The mirrors nd steel sheets obscure the edges of the conservatory, creating an lusion of an endless reflecting room, with the trapezoidal shape f the conservatory apparently expanded to seem almost like an ctagonal room with several dining tables and plants.

This is a stylish urban space, so the metal, glass, wood, and hite theme transfers easily from inside to outside, with the metal- nd-glass floor and table echoing the steel and glass structure.

inside

The addition of the conservatory increased the square footage of the main living area by about 25 percent, as well as making the room lighter and more flexible. The apartment is in a fashionable part of town, where the cost of property is high, so every spare inch is a bonus. This main room functions as a kitchen, living room, and, before the conservatory was added, also a dining area. The kitchen is at the back, and is the link between the conservatory and the main living area, while at the other end of the room are chairs, a sofa, and a fireplace. The soft furnishings fit into the metal, glass, wood, and white theme by being upholstered either in white or in fabrics and colors that evoke wood or metal: plain but handsome grays, plus shades of fawn, biscuit, and honey that evoke natural wood.

The kitchen area is a tiny square at the back of the room, but still manages to house a large steel refrigerator, a big cooktop and oven, and masses of storage space. The priority was to design cabinetry that concealed the mess of food preparation and dirty dishes, while allowing the cook to chat either to friends in the main room or to join in the conservatory conversation. This is achieved by double-sided cabinets: one side is higher and opens

1: A wall of glass bricks separates the hallway from the kitchen in order to maximise light.

2: The metal sink faces out onto the conservatory, offering a chance to chat while preparing food or washing up.

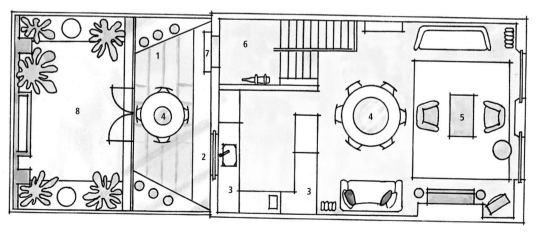

FLOORPLAN
(1) Sheets of toughened glass, bolted to hidden steel joists. (2) Former kitchen window, now removed to create open hatchway and improve air flow. (3) Kitchen cabinets. (4) Summer and winter positions for dining table. (5) Living area. (6) Stairway connecting main room and conservatory to the other floor. (7) Former door to stairway, now removed. (8) Patio.

on the living side, holding china and glass, while the other, with
kitchen equipment, is lower and opens on the kitchen side. The
countertop on this side is therefore hidden from view. Speakers
for a stereo system, which are concealed on either side of the
extractor fan, are insulated to give them the necessary protection
from the heat. Hanging rails, to hold different types of cooking
implements, and high-level shelves for pans ensure that no space
at all is wasted on the walls. Even the stairway is made to
work hard as it contains a steel wine rack that runs right from the
floor up to the ceiling.

above left: A high steel
cabinet hides food preparation
from the view of the diners,
and the cabinet beside it
opens onto both the kitchen
and dining area.

above: The steel, wood, and
glass theme, even for pots and
pans, prevents the cooking
zone from looking cluttered.

"Paris café" chairs

collapsible fabric loungers

Folding furniture saves space and is easy to move around, while pieces that look equally good inside or outside offer the maximum flexibility, and also maintain the links between house and garden. Shapes and styles can be traditional or modern – remember that you don't have to be limited by conventional conservatory furniture.

relaxed, versatile tables and chairs

haker-style storage

circular table

Use texture as a visual link between inner and outer spaces. Natural materials or neutral finishes – such as wood, stone, metal, and brick – will echo the colors and materials of the natural world outside, punctuated by brilliant splashes of color inside or flowers outside.

etal and wood for lighter looks

stone or terra-cotta floors

vinyl and linoleum

Geometric patterns can be found in stone or terra-cotta flooring, in vinyls or linoleum, and in textured wool, sisal, and seagrass. Textured or patterned flooring minimizes the effect of muddy footsteps, providing a durable, hard-wearing, and beautiful solution. Remember that sunlight can cause conservatory flooring to fade.

pendant lighting

seagrass, sisal, jute, and wool

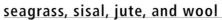

irework pendants

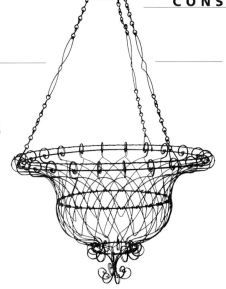

lantern lighting

etal and clay

Vertical shapes in the form of pendant baskets, pots, candles, lanterns, and lights, define the space. Repetition – two baskets, three candles, four pots – creates a sense of unity. Different shapes and styles can be drawn together by a theme of metal, terracotta or wire.

candles in pots

how to get the work done

Decorating a house involves commissioning a range of craftsmen, from plumbers, painters, and builders to architects, furniture makers and restorers. Finding the right person to do the work is rarely easy, but it is always worth taking the extra time to contact at least three different companies to compare quotations, and to discuss their ideas. It's also extremely difficult to guarantee the quality of the work, although the steps below should help minimize the chance of problems.

The most important point to remember is that it is your house, and you will have to live with their work. Your perspective is not the same as the workmen, craftsmen, and professionals you commission, and this can give you insights that they don't have. You owe it to yourself – and them – to stay in touch with ongoing work, to be clear about telling them what is most important to you, to take extra time to check every stage, not to assume anything – especially not that they can read your mind – and to make sure that they listen to your ideas. This doesn't mean turning yourself into the client from hell – a clear brief and a proper time frame, along with a fair structure of payment, will be welcomed by any true professional.

■ Look for professionals, craftsmen or workmen who specialize in the kind of work you want carried out. For example, architects who work on old buildings, or interior decorators experienced in country style or urban chic. The associations (see opposite) often keep lists of specific experts, and may also have "briefing guidelines" they can send you. Word of mouth, local directories, and newspapers are also good sources.

■ Look at past work or discuss former projects to ensure that you like their style. If you want an ultra-modern look, there's no point in commissioning a traditional designer, for example.

■ Explain what you have in mind and what your budget is. Give a clear idea of your daily life, how you live, and what you wish the work to achieve.

■ Write your brief down. Make sure that what you are asking can be understood – "stunningly beautiful but practical" does not mean much, while "pared-down country style with all domestic equipment concealed, yet easy to reach" gives a clear direction.

■ It is critical to check all plans and measurements in a way that makes sense to you. If the plans say 15 ft (3 m), for example, measure that out on the floor and see if it is the size you had envisaged. Check the size, style, and position of anything major, eg doors, windows, or radiators – ensuring the plans allows you flexibility when you come to furnishing. Mistakes are often made at this stage, and are expensive to correct once the work is done!

■ Be realistic about the time frame. Commissioning work is not the same as buying something from a shop – it will be weeks or months, not days. However, do make calls regularly to check progress and start or delivery dates. It helps prevent your job being sidelined for something more "urgent."

■ When restoring antiques or architectural salvage, don't risk amateur repairs. These can permanently damage the value. Find

t all you can, and look for experts. Specialist departments of
ction houses sometimes offer advice on whether repairs are
ssible without affecting the value, and may know suitable
ecialists you could contact.

Try out all colors, paints and wallpapers first in the largest
ssible patches or swatches on the wall to see what they look like
your room. Give yourself time to decide. If you're not clear
out what something looks like (eg low voltage halogen lighting,
ecialist wood veneers), see if you can find an example in a
end's house or showroom roomset.

■ Ask for a scale of fees and a formal quotation of what the work
will cost, and, if the initial plans and drawings are detailed, be
prepared to pay for these separately. If you go ahead, the cost will
often be deducted from the final bill. Work should be paid for in
instalments – a deposit, money for materials, more as stages are
completed, etc. Never pay the full amount upfront. Keep a small
percentage back for "snagging" – in other words, don't pay the
last amount until you have done a final thorough check of the
work. Then pay in full promptly. Most people work for themselves
or for small companies, and cash flow is critical to their survival.

seful addresses:

he American Crafts Council
2 Spring Street
ew York,
Y 10012-4019
l: 212 274 0630
formation on contemporary
afts in the U.S.

merican Friends of the
eorgian Group
o Ralph Harvard
77 East 70th Street
ew York,
Y 10021
l: 212 861 3990
aflets, trips and lectures on
storing Georgian properties.

merican Institute of
rchitects
735 New York Avenue NW
ashington,
C, 20006
l: 202 626 7300
sts of architects and
eir specialities.

The American Lighting
Association
World Trade Centre
Suite 10046
PO Box 420288
2050 Stemmons Freeway
Dallas,
TX 75342-0288
tel: 214 698 9898
fax: 214 698 9899
Members are lighting
manufacturers nationwide.

American Society of Interior
Designers
608 Massachussetts
Avenue NE
Washington,
DC 20002
tel: 202 546 3480
fax: 202 546 3240
www.asidnews.com
Listings of interior designers
and decorators.

Antique and Collectables
Dealer Association
c/o Jim Tucker
PO Box 2963
Huntersville,
NC 28070
tel: 704 895 9088
Advice on buying antiques,
details of members.

Antique Dealers' Association
of America, Inc.
PO Box 335
Greens Farms,
CT 06436
fax: 203 255 3197
Advice on buying antiques,
details of members.

Art and Antique Dealers
League of America, Inc
353 East 78th Street
Suite 19A
New York,
NY 10021
tel: 212 879 7558
Non-profit membership
organization devoted to
dealers and buyers of
antiques and works of art,
and to the encouragement of
educational and cultural
activities in the arts.

The Victorian Society
in America
c/o the Secretary
The Athenaeum
219 South 6th Street
Philadelphia,
PA 19106
tel: 215 627 4252
fax: 215 627 7221
www.libertynet.org/vicsoc
Information on Victorian
features, and all aspects of
preserving original
Victorian architecture.

directory

Furniture, lighting, storage, bedding, and china simil
to the items featured on the "Creating the look" pag
can be obtained from the companies in this director
and the architects and designers who worked on th
various homes are also listed here. As stock chang
regularly, we have not specified exactly where eac
item came from, but if you want to buy similar piece
this directory lists the company speciality under th
address. Those that do not have formal mail ord
catalogs will usually ship items nationwide whe
specified, and you can check in the Mail Order sectic
for those offering full mail order services.

NTIQUES

he American Wing
415 Main Street
ridgehampton,
IY 11932
el: 516 537 3319

.my Perlin Antiques
06 East 61st St.
th Fl.
Iew York,
IY 10021
el: 212 593 5756

.uby Beets
703 Montauk Highway
.ridgehampton,
IY 14873
el: 516 537 2802

.age Street Antiques
.age Street
.ag Harbour,
IY 11963
el: 516 725 4036

BATHROOM SPECIALISTS

Bed, Bath & Beyond
620 Avenue of the Americas
New York,
NY 10011
Tel: 212 255 3550
Also for kitchenware, window
hardware and various home
accessories

Portico Bed & Bath
139 Spring Street
New York,
NY 10012
Tel: 212 941 7722
Bed and bath linen, kimonos and
a selection of toiletries

BEDS AND BEDDING

Cuddledown of Maine
Tel: 800 323 6793
Mail order catalog

United Feather & Down
Factory Outlet Store
414 East Gulf Road
Des Plaines,
IL 60016
Tel: 800 932 DOWN
Wide range of bedding including
pillows and comforters

CONSERVATORIES AND GARDENS

Charleston Gardens
61 Queen Street
Charleston,
SC 29401
Tel: 803 723 0252
Garden furniture and accessories

Rooms and Gardens
290 Lafayette Street
New York,
NY 10012
Tel: 212 431 1297
Garden furniture and accessories

Smith & Hawken
Two Arbor Lane
Box 6900
Florence,
KY 41022 6900 (distribution center)
Tel: 800 776 3336
Catalog and stores nationwide—outdoor and indoor

PAINT AND TILES

Benjamin Moore
31 Chestnut Ridge Road
Montvale,
NJ 07645
Tel: 1 888 236 6667
Interior and exterior paint

Crossville Ceramics
PO Box 1168
Crossville,
TN 38557
Tel: 931 484 2110
Tiles

Glidden Company
Tel: 800 221 4100
Interior and exterior paints

Liberty Paint Company
969 Columbia Street
Hudson,
NY 12534
Tel: 518 828 4060
Interior and exterior paints

FURNITURE STORES

Cassina
155 East 56th Street
New York,
NY 10022
Tel: 516 423 4560
Contemporary, country, and classic ranges

Aero
132 Spring Street
New York,
NY 10012
Tel: 212 966 1500
Eclectic—moderne and classic

The Bombay Company
Tel: 800 829 7789
Stores nationwide and catalog—traditional and country

City Barn Antiques
269 Lafayette Street
New York,
NY 10012
Tel: 718 855 8566
Blondewood, Heywood-Wakefield furniture

Coconut Company
131 Greene Street
New York,
NY 10012
Tel: 212 559 1940
Far Eastern and European furnishings

elaware River Trading Company
5 Trenton Avenue
renchtown,
J 08825
el: 800 732 4791
ountry furniture and accessories,
ew and old

ialogica
84 Broome Street
ew York,
Y 10013
el: 212 966 1934

so at
394 Melrose Avenue
os Angeles,
A 90069
el: 213 951 1993
ofas, chairs, tables, and rugs

oor Store
00 433 4071
ontemporary, country, and
lassic

nside Out
1 Railroad Avenue
ast Hampton,
Y 11937
el: 516 329 3600
lassic furniture

The Lively Set
33 Bedford Street
New York,
NY 10014
Tel: 212 807 8417
Eclectic and American country
furniture

Lost City Arts
275 Lafayette Street
New York,
NY 10012
Tel: 212 941 8025
American 20th century
furniture and fixtures

Luminaire
301 West Superior
Chicago,
IL 60610
Tel: 312 664 9581
European contemporary
furniture, lighting, and
accessories

Modern Age
102 Wooster Street
New York,
NY 10003
Tel: 212 966 0669
Modern design

Moss
146 Greene Sreet
New York,
NY 10012
Tel: 212 226 2190
Modern furniture, housewares,
lighting, and tableware

Nancy Sach Gallery
7700 Forsyth
St. Louis,
MO 63105
Tel: 314 727 7770
Contemporary furniture and
crafts by American artisans

Palecek
P.O. Box 2256
Richmond,
CA 94808-0225
Tel: 800 274 7730
Wicker furniture, baskets,
and accessories, directory
to stores

Troy
138 Greene Street
New York,
NY 10012
Tel: 212 941 4777
Modern and classic furniture
and accessories

Zona
97 Greene Street
New York,
NY 10012
Tel: 212 925 6750
Classic and country: Italian and
Southwestern

Maine Cottage
PO Box 935
Yarmouth,
ME 04096
Painted country furniture

Norwalk Furniture
100 Furniture Parkway
Norwalk,
OH 44857
Tel: 800 837 2565
Classic upholstered pieces

HOME STORES

ABC Carpet & Home
888 Broadway
New York,
NY 10003
Tel: 212 473 3000
Period furniture, as well as bath
and kitchen accessories

Calvin Klein home
For nationwide stores
tel: 800 294 7978
Pure minimalist furniture,
tableware, bed, and bath linens
and accessories

Crate & Barrel
650 Madison Avenue
New York,
NY 10022
Tel: 212 294 0011
For nationwide stores
tel: 800 996 9960
Simple, clean designs for
furniture and accessories

Ikea
Twelve stores: Philadelphia
(Plymouth Meeting, PA);
Washington (Woodbridge, VA);
Baltimore; Pittsburgh, Elizabeth
NJ; New York (Hicksville, NY);
Houston; Burbank CA; Tustin CA
Industry CA; Carson CA; Seattle
(Renton, WA)
tel: 410 931 8940, 800 434 4532
For customer service:
626 912 1119
Swedish furniture group known
for its well-priced self-assembly
furniture and accessories for all
rooms in the house

Laura Ashley
For nationwide stores
tel: 800 367 2000
Fashion and furnishings,
fabric, china, and bathroom
accessories

Pier One
461 Fifth Avenue
New York,
NY 10017
Tel: 212 447 1610
For nationwide stores
tel: 800 447 4371 or see
www. pier1.com
Casual furniture, rattan, and
iron plus some dining and
tableware and picnic
accessories

Portico Home
2 Spring Street
New York,
NY 10012
Tel: 212 941 7800
Dining and bedroom
furniture, lighting, and
upholstery. An eclectic mix
of both modern and classic
designs in simple natural
colors

Pottery Barn
965 Broadway
New York,
NY 10023
For nationwide stores
Tel: 800 922 5507

Takashimaya
693 Fifth Avenue
New York,
NY 10022
Tel: 212 350 0100
        800 753 2038
Japanese department store
with flower shop, furniture
and accessories

KITCHEN SPECIALISTS

Dean & Deluca
560 Broadway
New York,
NY 10012
Tel: 212 226 6800
Mail order : 800 221 7714,
800 999 0306
A deli-coffee bar with a
comprehensive cookware
department

William Sonoma
800 541 2233
Cookware (stores nationwide)

LIGHTING

Gailbraith & Paul
307 North Third Street
Philadelphia,
PA 19106
Tel: 215 923 4632
Lamps and bases

Just Shades
21 Spring Street
New York,
NY 10012
Tel: 212 966 2757
Lampshades

Sirmos
979 Third Avenue
New York,
NY 10022
Tel: 718 786 5920
Contemporary lighting

MAIL ORDER

Crate & Barrel
PO Box 9059
Wheeling,
IL 60090-9059 (mail order)
Tel: 800 451 8217

Pottery Barn
PO Box 7044
San Francisco,
CA 94120-7044
Tel: 800 922 5507

Hold Everything
PO Box 7807
San Francisco,
CA 94120
Tel: 800 421 2264

Bauer International
414 Jessen Lane
Wando,
SC 29492
Tel: 843 884 4007
Indonesian plantation furniture

MIRRORS, PICTURES AND DECORATIVE ACCESSORIES

Kate's Paperie
561 Broadway
New York,
NY 10012
Tel: 941 9816
Wallpaper, paper furnishings
for the home, stationery

Ad Hoc Softwares
410 W. Broadway
New York,
NY 10021
Tel: 212 925 2652
Contemporary tableware,
bed and bath linen

Design Ideas
PO Box 2967
Springfield,
IL 62708
For nationwide stores
tel: 217 753 3081
Contemporary bathroom
accessories, home office,
storage, picture frames, wall
screens

Wolfman Gold & Good Co.
117 Mercer Street
New York,
NY 10012
Tel: 212 966 7055
Classic range of tableware
and linen

STORAGE

The Container Store
7700 West Northwest Highway
Ste. 500
Dallas,
TX 75225 (flagship store)

also at
2000 Valwood Parkway
Dallas, TX 75234 (mail order)
Tel: 800 733 3532
A huge range of storage goods
for the home

Hold Everything
Second & 69th Street
New York,
NY 10021
Tel: 212 535 9446
An extensive range of storage
accessories for the bedroom,
bathroom, and kitchen

OFT FURNISHINGS

esigner's Guild
a Osborne & Little
0 Commerce Road
amford,
T 06902
or nationwide stockists
l: 203 359 1500
brics and wallpapers

Schumacher & Company
39 Third Aveune
t 56th Street)
ew York,
Y 10022
el: 800 988 7775
Vall coverings, fabrics and rugs

sborne & Little
79 Third Avenue
ew York,
Y 10022
el: 203 359 1500
Vall coverings and fabrics

Vaverly Home
9 Madison Avenue
14th Fl.)
ew York,
Y 10016
el: 800 423 5881
Vall coverings and fabrics

FURNITURE
MANUFACTURERS

Drexel Heritage
800 916 1986
Traditional. National listing
of dealers

Ethan Allen Home Interiors
Tel: 800 228 9229
Contemporary, country, and
traditional

Grange
Tel: 800 GRANGE 1
French country and traditional

Henredon
800-444 3682
www.henredon.com
Traditional

Lane
Tel: 800 544 4694
Traditional

Lexington
800 544 4694
Traditional

The Mitchell Gold Company
P.O. Box 819
Taylorsville,
NC 28681
Tel: 800 789 5401
Classic upholstered pieces

Thomasville
Tel: 800 927 9202
www.thomasville.com
Traditional

index

Page numbers in bold refer to refer to illustrations.